M…

A GUIDE … STORY
OF THE A… OREST

text
MATT BANNERMAN
based on information
from Mamirauá contributors

photos
LUIZ CLAUDIO MARIGO

Instituto de
Desenvolvimento Sustentável Mamirauá
IDSM

Contributors from Mamirauá

Aline Da Rin P. Azevêdo
Andréa Pires
Anthony Martin
Augusto Fachin Teran
Edila A. Moura
Helder L. Queiroz
José Márcio Ayres
Leandro Castello
Luiz Claudio Marigo
Marinus Hoogmoed
Nelissa P. Bezerra
Ronis da Silveira
Teresa Cristina Avila-Pires
Vera Silva
William Crampton
William Hamilton

Instituto de Desenvolvimento Sustentável Mamirauá - IDSM

Sponsors

Ministério da Ciência e Tecnologia - MCT
Department for International Development - DFID
Wildlife Conservation Society - WCS
European Union - EU
Instituto de Proteção Ambiental do Estado do Amazonas - IPAAM

With the purchase of this book you are making a contribution to the establishment of Mamirauá Sustainable Development Reserve.

FOREWORD

This Guidebook presents the flooded forests of Mamirauá Reserve in all their glory.

Certainly one of the most beautiful sites in the Amazon, Mamirauá is one of the few places in that region where important species of *flora* and *fauna* of the complex ecosystem of the *várzea* are still abundant and can be actually observed by anyone.

Throughout this Guidebook, Mamirauá's exuberance is presented to its visitors in magnificent photographs and short but comprehensive text, compiled from fresh information provided by many scientific experts working in the area for years. The chapters are organised especially to make available for all readers and future visitors, whatever their background, the huge amount of information gathered from the amazing landscape of Mamirauá flooded forest and its plants and animals.

But Mamirauá is much more than exotic primates, enormous black caimans, graceful river dolphins, gigantic fish or large areas of luxuriant, annually flooded forest. The Mamirauá Reserve is also an officially protected conservation unit, where the local community is implementing the sustainable use of natural resources, and adopting new economic activities with a low environmental impact. The reader will find in this Guidebook chapters explaining this very unusual conservation strategy and the traditional population inhabiting the *várzea* as well.

The present Guidebook is the result of the efforts of many people working for the conservation of Mamirauá. Scientific experts, photographers, writers and many others were involved in the organisation of this Guide. But the final product, in the form of this book, is mostly a result of the efforts of those working in the Eco-tourism group.

In the search for a more environmentally based model of community development, Mamirauá's Program of Eco-tourism has been implemented since 1997. This program provides an alternative source of income to support the management of the Reserve, and supports the livelihoods for part of its traditional population. Mamirauá Eco-tourism now opens the Reserve's breathtaking landscapes to tourists, guests and other visitors.

Welcome to Mamirauá Reserve!

CP 38 - CEP 69470-000 - Tefé - Amazonas - Brazil
Phone/fax + 55 (92) 343-2736

Production:
Marigo Comunicação Visual Ltda.

Design:
Cecília Banhara Marigo

Captions originally written in Portuguese:
Luiz Claudio Marigo

Captions translation:
Dorothy Sue Dunn de Araujo

CATALOGAÇÃO NA FONTE DO
DEPARTAMENTO NACIONAL DO LIVRO

B219m
Bannerman, Matt.
Mamirauá : a guide to the natural history of the amazon flooded forest / text Matt Bannerman ; photos Luiz Claudio Marigo. – Tefé : IDSM, 2001.
176 p. : il. ; 22,5 cm.

ISBN 85-88758-02-4

Inclui bibliografia.

1. Reserva natural de Mamirauá (AM) I. Instituto de Desenvolvimento Sustentável Mamirauá. II. Título.

CDD-918.1

Cover:
Mamirauá Lake, Amazon water lily (*Victoria amazonica*), White-uakari (*Cacajau calvus calvus*), Flower of mungubarana tree (*Pachira aquatica*).

Following pages:
6/7 Bird's-eye view of the Mamirauá Sustainable Development Reserve, showing the lakes and the *chavascal* and *restinga* vegetation.
8/9 Scarlet macaws (*Ara macao*) flying over the flooded forest.
10/11 Hoatzins (*Opisthocomus hoazin*) basking in the sun on the shores of Mamirauá Lake.
12/13 Large-billed terns (*Phaetusa simplex*) on the banks of the Japurá River. In the dry season, they nest on the beaches exposed by the receding waters.

CONTENTS

WELCOME TO MAMIRAUÁ

Bem-vindo ao Mamirauá! The engine cuts out, and the launch drifts in silence towards the floating lodge. You loosen the straps on your life jacket, adjust to the stillness after the bouncing motion of the speedboat, maybe even run a hand through hair blown about by your rapid progress on the open waterway. With the breeze gone the sun is hot, though to the west, over the trees that line the bank, afternoon clouds are piling up. Behind the lodge a hawk screams, once. Grumbles of far-off thunder mix with a strange chorus that swells suddenly from the forest on all sides, like a hundred children swinging on a hundred rusty gates. '*Guariba*', says a friendly face, reaching down to take your pack and give you a hand up onto the deck. 'Howler monkey. *Bem-vindo*, welcome, to Mamirauá.'

A thousand miles from the mouth of the Amazon, a thousand more from its source in the Andes: look for Mamirauá on the map and you will find it right at the heart of the world's greatest river basin. North and south from here the forest stretches away to the borders with Venezuela and Bolivia. Westward the riverboats chug upstream to Colombia and Peru, five days journey. East the river flows toward Belém and the distant Atlantic, joined amidst a confusing jumble of islands by its tributary the Japurá. Between the two rivers lies the Mamirauá Sustainable Development Reserve, known more simply as Mamirauá, and this book is an introduction to its rivers, lakes, swamps and flooded forests, and the people, animals and plants who inhabit them. Mamirauá is a world of water, sky and forest, beautiful and strange, frustrating and fascinating. And yet just this morning you were in Manaus.

Squatting at the confluence of the Amazon with its largest tributary, the Rio Negro, Amazonia's most populous city has had a roller coaster history. Filled with riches by the rubber boom and drained just as quickly by the crash, Manaus is now sprawling again, its economic pump primed by sweeping tax-breaks and the status of a free-trade zone that is always just about to be suspended. The Eduardo Gomes international airport is the main gateway to the Brazilian Amazon, and most travellers will spend a night in the city. A tour of the town can be enlightening, if only to

The peace and beauty of sunsets on Mamirauá Lake are enjoyed by all Reserve visitors.

see at first hand the end point of the chain of rural migration and urban development that has shaped the recent history of the region. Manaus folk are busy, enterprising and engaging people. But faced with the array of curio shops and jungle tours, better to keep your wallet in your pocket and head west. Next to Eduardo Gomes, its little brother airport, Eduardinho, is the base for most of the short flights to Tefé.

For such an expansive city, Manaus falls away remarkably quickly once your plane lifts off the ground and banks out across the Rio Negro. There is little in the way of suburb: on this side of the city the forest closes in quickly, and below your window the view is soon an uninterrupted carpet of green, the canopy from the air looking like nothing so much as a huge head of broccoli extending to the horizon in every direction. On clear days, which depending on the season may be rare indeed over the rainforest, the scale of the view from ten thousand feet can be dizzying. Rainforest streams wind their way sinuously across the scene, each meander flashing gold in turn with reflected sunlight. In the wet season, the sun itself can be a constant companion, a flickering disc chasing the plane's shadow through the forest, reflected in floodwaters beneath the canopy. More likely, however, the trees are only glimpsed through the clouds, wispy cumulus that build through the afternoon into giant thunderheads many thousands of feet high that the plane weaves through as if in another forest in the sky.

Down there somewhere, throughout the flight, is the great river itself, picked up just out from Manaus: sometimes a broad chocolate ribbon out on the right; sometimes a dozen fragmented strands choked with forested islands to the left, but always there. From the air you begin to see what a complex system the Amazon floodplain really is: a maze of tributaries, levees, sandbanks and lakes of different colours. The origins of this confusing and beautiful landscape are the subject of Chapter 2. But now one of the lakes is coming up to meet you and on a promontory, overlooking the water, you can make out the roofs and towers of Tefé.

Picked up in a four-wheel drive vehicle at the airport, the short trip into town to the port is the only section of your journey to be by road. The bustling streets of Tefé are an illusion: every one of the cars and ubiquitous motorbikes has been brought in by boat. The few roads that leave town peter out after a few kilometres, at the airport or at agricultural settlements, and the forest reasserts itself. Rivers are the arteries of the upper Amazon, and the true heart of the town is down by the waterfront. Here is the market, full of strange Amazonian fish and fruits as well as plastic sandals (useful) and spandex hot pants (less useful). Down at the dock, the riverboats are tied up six deep to floating quays, rocking gently in the waves the afternoon breeze brings in off the lake. The three decked *Capitão Nunes*, just in from Manaus, is being unloaded, a chain of men emerging from the hold with sacks of sugar on their heads and slapping in sandaled feet across a perilous plank onto the beach. Beyond, a board slung from the bridge of the *Alves Filho* announces that she leaves

Bird's-eye view of the Amazon River in the dry season near the town of Tefé.

Bird's-eye view of Tefé, the starting point for all trips to the Mamirauá Reserve, in the dry season.

One of the old sapucaia trees of Boca do Mamirauá, in the dry and the flood seasons.

for the border town of Tabatinga at five o'clock. Her only deck is already filling up; the hammocks slung two and three deep as families arrange themselves and their belongings for the long days on the river.

Around and between the large boats there is constant canoe traffic. Long craft bump alongside piled high with ice boxes of fish or sacks of manioc flour, their *rabeta* outboard motors pop-popping as the helmsman aims for the few unoccupied feet of landing space. Another is leaving, low in the water with the month's provisions and three little girls perched on top of the coffee and soap, sheltering from the sun under a black umbrella. Smaller still, the dugout canoes are piloted by lone men in the bows, dipping their paddles in economical strokes, headed out into the lake. And the boy selling frozen fruit squash from a styrofoam box around his neck perches on just a plank of driftwood, another plank his paddle. But soon the Ecotourism launch pulls up, luggage and supplies are loaded, and you are nosing out into open water, where the driver can open up the throttle.

Close to town, the banks are crowded with *flutuantes*, floating buildings selling ice or buying fish, floating mechanics, even floating gas stations. But as the church tower of Santa Teresa drops out of sight behind, the habitations thin out. One or two wealthy citizens have comfortable weekend retreats, and wire fences mark the pasture where cattle are raised to provide Tefé's beef. On the southern side of the channel, the land rises steeply: the edge of the *terra firme*, the solid land that will stay dry when the rivers rise in the flood season. These red soil escarpments are dotted with tall and elegant *castanheiras*, the trees that yield the *castanha-do-Pará*, better known abroad as the Brazil nut. Across the river, the ground is lower but thickly covered with different species of tree and shrub. This is the beginning of the *várzea*, the flooded forests, annually inundated to depths of thirty feet or more, when a sheet of water can extend for twenty miles unbroken across the floodplain. The boat swings over and heads for the *várzea* bank, and the driver raises his hand to point. *'Água branca',* he says. 'White water'.

The water issuing from the small cut that the bows now point at is not white, but certainly very different from the dark waters of Lago Tefé. The current spills out in eddies the colour of milk chocolate or café au lait, and meeting the lake water swirls in intricate patterns as the two streams blend and move away downstream. This is Tefé's very own *encontro das águas*, or meeting of the waters, a miniature version of the Manaus tourist attraction, where the Rio Negro meets the main stream. You cross the watery boundary and plunge into the cut, the driver needing all his skill to weave between the branches, trunks and other debris that are suddenly everywhere. On the larger logs, terns perch and watch you go by. Ahead, the mouth of the cut widens and the banks fall away, until met by a gust of wind and an extra chop to the water you emerge into the main stream of the Amazon itself.

Two things are immediately confusing. First of all the stretch of river between

A group of American students, on their way to walk a forest trail.

One of the modules of the Uakari Floating Lodge and its interior. Lodging at Mamirauá is simple, but comfortable, and well adapted to the ecological reality of the flooded-forest.

the mouth of the Negro at Manaus and the Peru/Colombia border is always known as the Rio Solimões. In Brazil, the name Rio Amazonas is only applied to the lower reaches. Secondly, this is not really the main stream; rather, it is one of several main streams. Close to Tefé, as in many other stretches along its length, the Solimões is divided by islands into several channels, creating a navigational maze through which only the experienced can pick their way. Rarely do you get an impression of the full extent of the river. But what you see is impressive enough. For the next half an hour, the boat hugs the bank to take advantage of the slacker current, whilst forest on the far shore advances and recedes but is seldom closer than a mile of choppy, muddy water away. You might be in the estuary of one of the world's great rivers. But the water churning past is fresh. The sea is a thousand miles away.

The first sighting of river dolphins presages your arrival at the Boca do Mamirauá. The *bocas*, or mouths, of *várzea* lake systems are favourite hunting grounds for the top predators of the river, and two dolphin backs rise in sedate succession. The spray of their exhalations can be seen, though the trademark 'huff' is lost under the note of the engine. But there is no mistaking the fact that they are bright pink: these are boto, wonderfully adapted for life in the *várzea* lake and channels and the stuff of legend for the people who live here. There is little but the presence of the dolphins to give away the narrow opening in the tall *capim* grass, and for a moment they are all around the boat, but then they are left behind as you are through the gap and the little community of the Boca appears, perched on a high levee in the shade of two spreading *sapucaia* trees.

With a wave of an arm and a shout the boat is beckoned over to one of the small timber houses and the cause is soon apparent: a huge, strange fish is hauled aboard. 'Dinner!' grins the woman who follows the fish over the gunwale, wearing a Mamirauá T-shirt and smiling *'Boa tarde!'* The nearby communities provide the guides and cooks for the ecotourism operation, as well as fresh fish for the lodge kitchen. Gliding on into the forest, the water is mirror smooth, broken only by the rising of fish and rafts of floating water grasses lazily descending on the current. A heron starts from the bank and flaps ahead of the boat, and up ahead, afloat on the edge of a broad pool where the stream doubles back on itself, is the Uakari Lodge.

Journey's end, and the beginning of an exploration that we hope this book will guide. The chapters that follow offer an introduction to the *várzea* and its inhabitants. However, your trip will no doubt be different. Mamirauá seldom presents the same face: the changing flora and fauna and above all the rise and fall of the waters can transform your surroundings overnight. As we shall see, this is a highly dynamic environment, and the adaptation to its demands by the plants, animals and people who make their home here is at the core of the remarkable story of the flooded forest. There is always something going on.

Bem-vindo ao Mamirauá.

THE MAMIRAUÁ SUSTAINABLE DEVELOPMENT RESERVE

The early days in Mamirauá

Two characters dominate the short but eventful history of the Mamirauá reserve, and they could hardly be more different. One is short of stature, shy and as pale as any Englishman, save for a dyspeptic scarlet visage glimpsed occasionally through the branches of the Mamirauá trees. The other stands more than six feet tall, is gregarious and genial by nature and shows in a tanned face the legacy of many years spent peering up, notebook and binoculars in hand, into those same trees. The white uakari, sometimes called the English monkey after its peculiar complexion, is found only in the *várzea* flooded forests enclosed by the Solimões and Japurá rivers and the Auati-Paraná canal. Primatologist Dr. Jose Márcio Ayres, on the other hand, is today a globetrotting ambassador and fund-raiser for those forests and the unique conservation unit that protects them: the Mamirauá Sustainable Development Reserve.

As recently as the 1980's, the only description of the uakari *Cacajao calvus calvus* in its natural habitat was contained in the notes of the English naturalist Henry Walter Bates, who lived in nearby Tefé in the middle years of the nineteenth century and made extensive studies of the flora and fauna of the seasonally flooded forests that extend along the Solimões and its tributaries. With his departure, the white uakari went unstudied for close to a hundred and fifty years, until March of 1983, when Ayres, a young biologist from the state of Pará, at the mouth of the Amazon, set out from Tefé in an old boat partly paid for by his parents, to look for the mysterious scarlet faced monkey. Abandoning several field sites as too remote, driven from others by the ferocity of the insects, he finally pointed his boat the *Gaivota* into the narrow mouth of the Mamirauá lake system. 'All along our route a great variety of floating meadows and other aquatic plants navigating discretely over the black waters, between flocks of egrets, ducks, herons and cormorants. Coming from the banks the calls of kingfishers, herons and, not uncommonly, squirrel monkeys.'

Dr. José Márcio Ayres and the white uakari, the two main characters responsible for the creation of the Mamirauá Reserve. One has studied the other…

Today's visitor to Mamirauá has much the same impressions, though in a slightly higher degree of comfort. In those pioneering days, a shoestring research budget tested the dedication of Ayres and his companions. Luiz Claudio Marigo, whose photographs illustrate this book, accompanied Ayres on some of his first expeditions. The *Gaivota* was slow, lacking in facilities and unsuited to the challenges of the climate. 'The boat was completely enclosed, and below decks where we slept it was a furnace. The only way to wash was to dive into the river with a bar of soap.' Trekking after the uakari, bivouacking in the forest, the two men subsisted on piranha and rice, or corned beef from the tin, their meals often snatched whilst the monkeys they were observing paused to feed themselves in a tree overhead.

The Mamirauá Reserve in Amazonas State.

José Márcio Ayres studying the ecology of the white uakari, at Mamirauá Lake, in 1985.

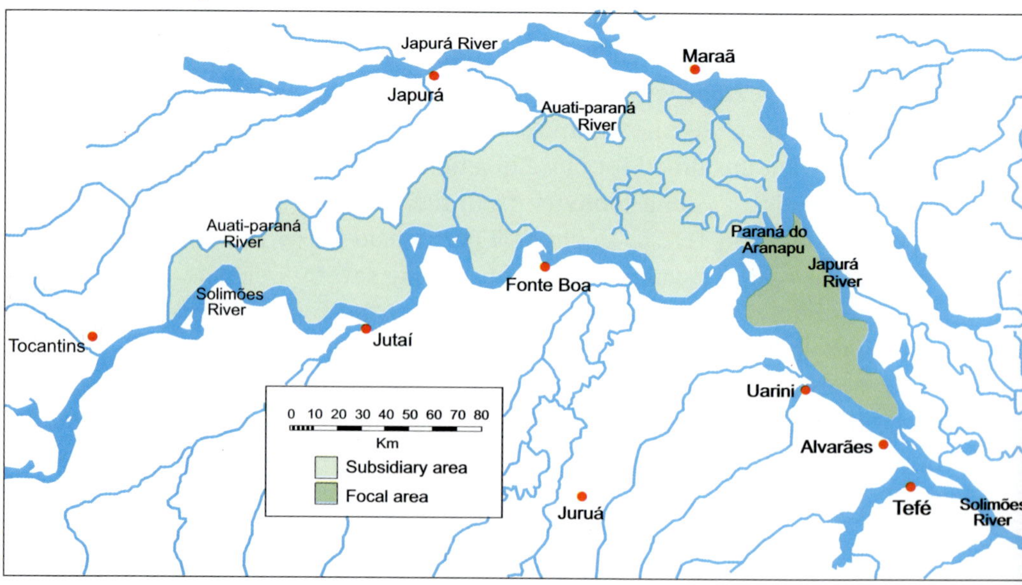

A map of the Focal Area and the Subsidiary Area of the Mamirauá Reserve.

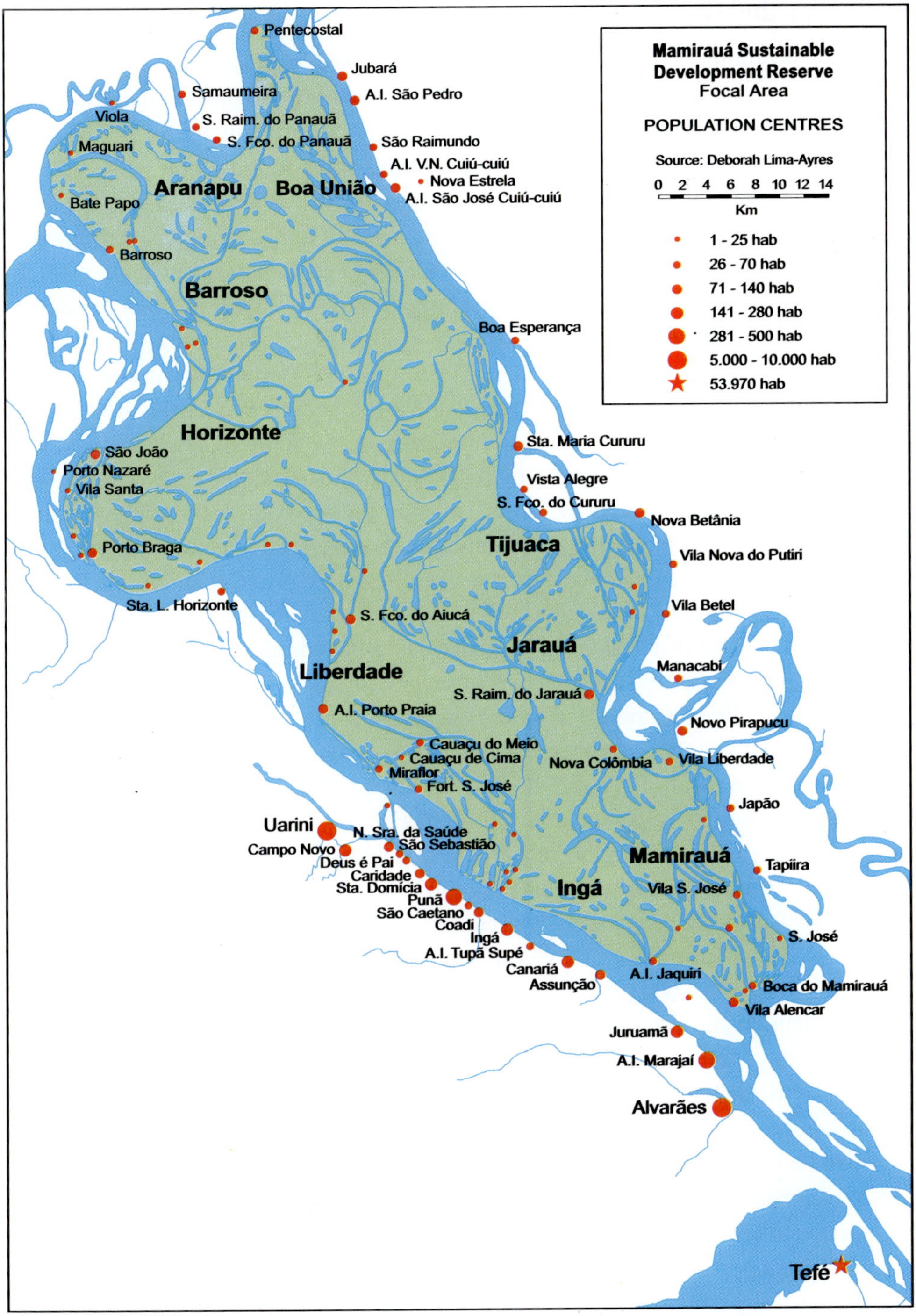

A map of settlement distribution in the Mamirauá Reserve (Focal Area).

Protection and threats

Ayres' groundbreaking study was published in 1986, and in 1990 over a million hectares of *várzea*, including the area in which his fieldwork had been carried out, was declared the Mamirauá Ecological Station by the government of the state of Amazonas. The new reserve protected the entire known range of the white uakari, as well as a new species of squirrel monkey that Ayres had described in 1985. Just as importantly, it became the first reserve to lie entirely within the unique environment of the *várzea* flooded forest. For reasons that will be discussed in Chapter 2, the *várzea* supports less biodiversity, at least among terrestrial species, than adjoining areas of *terra firme*, but is characterised by a high degree of endemism: species who are found here and nowhere else, as exemplified by the uakari. Further, the *várzea* aquatic systems are highly diverse, and astonishingly productive. Due to the annual nutrient replenishment with the flooding of the sediment-rich white water rivers, and the ideal reproductive habitat offered by the inundated forests during the flood season, the *várzea* acts as larder and nursery for countless species of fish, amongst which are some of the most important commercial species of the region.

But it is the very abundance of the *várzea* that may prove its undoing. As the urban centres of the Amazon continue to expand, so does the demand for cheap protein, and the fish of the rivers and *várzea* lakes have traditionally met this need. Over fishing is perhaps the most serious of several threats to the *várzea* at Mamirauá. In the lower reaches of the river, forest clearing for cattle pasture has been widespread, whilst other aquatic species such as turtles, manatees and caimans continue to be hunted for meat, eggs and skins, with little effective control. *Várzea* trees have value as timber, and selective felling has greatly reduced the populations of certain favoured species. In the face of these depletions, the establishment of the Ecological Station gave the natural wealth of the *várzea* a level of theoretical protection. But policing of such a large and remote area presents real problems. And there was a further complication: the new reserve was already the home of thousands of families who continued to survive in the traditional *ribeirinho* way, by growing manioc and catching fish. Would they have to leave?

Even today, many of the communities of Mamirauá are remote and unused to visitors, so the arrival in 1983 of the *Gaivota* and the tall stranger on board caused a considerable commotion. The first man Ayres hailed fled into the forest: later it emerged that he had taken the scientist for a policeman and hastened to dispose of a sack of turtles that represented his morning's work. The second thought he must be a priest, albeit one with odd ideas, and agreed to guide Ayres to the far end of Lago Mamirauá, where he made his first uakari observations. The Catholic Church had for several years been active in encouraging community organisation in these far-flung settlements. Now it looked as though a novel partnership between scientists and local people might emerge, to defend the *várzea* that played such a central role

The *Gaivota* helped Márcio Ayres' carry out his studies for his Ph.D. thesis. A gift from his father in 1983, Márcio donated it, in turn, to the Mamirauá Reserve where it provides support for other scientists to this day.

The arapaima is one of the Amazon's most important commercial fishes. Volunteer wardens from the Boca do Mamirauá settlement show dried, salted arapaima confiscated from poachers.

Intensive forestry research helps the river people exploit forest resources legally without interfering with the biodiversity. During the flood season, when fish populations disperse into the forest and fields lie underwater, timber exploitation is an important subsistence alternative.

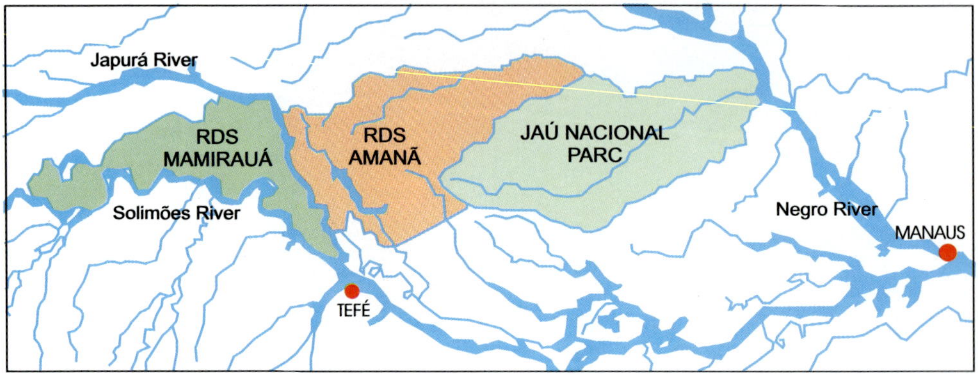

A map of the Central Amazon ecological corridor, joining the Mamirauá and Amanã Sustainable Development Reserves and Jaú National Park.

in sustaining their livelihoods. In 1992 the NGO Sociedade Civil Mamirauá was formed to co-ordinate research and extension work within the new reserve, and in 1996 a management plan was published which emphasised the importance of the role of local people, both in maintaining sustainable use of natural resources by themselves and their families, and in policing the remote corners of the reserve and preventing outsiders from breaking the rules governing the use of those resources. That same year the government of the state of Amazonas passed a law that enshrined these principles in the creation of a new and unique conservation unit, and the Mamirauá Sustainable Development Reserve came into existence. Today, the children and grandchildren of Ayres' original guide are actively involved in the protection and management of the *várzea* forest the two men explored together a generation ago.

How the Reserve works

Mamirauá Sector, in which the Ecotourism Zone is located, is only one of nine sectors that make up the Focal Area of the reserve. This in turn is only a part of the total area, a focus for limited resources and a model for development in the remainder of the reserve, known as the Subsidiary Area. The Mamirauá reserve itself provides a model for the new and neighbouring Amanã Sustainable Development Reserve, which links Mamirauá with Jaú National Park, creating the largest contiguous area of protected tropical forest in the world. The logistics are daunting. The *Gaivota* still plies to and from the reserve, though she is now supported by five other large boats and a fleet of twenty-seven aluminium speedboats, whilst ten floating houses provide field bases for Mamirauá staff, even at the height of the floods, and the radios they contain allow vital communication with the furthest corners of the reserve. Every afternoon, the reserve HQ in Tefé, a small house on the Avenida Brasil, crackles with reports and requests from the field, though static from frequent electric storms means that only expert ears can decipher them. Upstairs, along with a library, is a more sophisticated communication device: the only internet server for five hundred kilometres. This level of infrastructure is not cheap, and financial support comes from both the Brazilian government, via the National Council for Scientific and Technological Development (CNPq), and a group of international donors that include the Department for International Development (DFID) of the British Government, the Wildlife Conservation Society (WCS) in the US, and the European Union (EU).

At any moment, the Avenida Brasil house is likely to be full of scientists, both Brazilian and international, on their way to and from the forest. Ayres' work on the uakari was the first of many innovative research programs. Mamirauá has also seen the first ecological study of the pirarucu *Arapaima gigas*, the first radio tracking of freshwater dolphins and the first study of the magnificent and threatened black caiman in the wild. As well as a new species of primate, studies of the diverse aquatic systems have uncovered between fifteen and twenty species of electric fish previously unknown to science. Mamirauá has become one of the most studied stretches of *várzea* forest in the world, a centre of excellence in decoding the mysteries of the flooded forest.

Research is only part of the story, however. A whole range of activities, grouped under the heading 'extension', aim to assist the scattered *várzea* communities to organise for resource management and develop economic alternatives to unsustainable resource use. A health team advises on basic health precautions: environmental education workers raise awareness of the ecological issues bound up in *várzea* livelihoods. An agriculture project encourages experimentation with new and high yielding varieties of crop and fruit tree, whilst a timber project is training local people to draw up management plans to allow them to sustainably and legally exploit the timber resource around their communities. Women's groups are exploring the potential of marketing traditional crafts such as pottery and basketwork. A community radio program, broadcast twice a week, keeps the residents of the reserve abreast of the latest developments.

One of the most important dates in the Mamirauá calendar is the annual General Assembly. Delegates attend from all corners of the reserve, often travelling through the night to do so, and they are joined by representatives of the church, the army, the municipal government, the commercial fisherman's union and other important local organisations. For three days, the reserve and its management become the subject of intense dialogue, important decisions are made and controversial proposals are voted on. On the afternoon of the final day, the little fleet of boats returns with the delegates to their far-flung communities, where they begin the process of explaining and justifying the commitments they have entered into to their family and neighbours who remained at home.

THE VÁRZEA ECOSYSTEMS

Blue, black and white water: the prehistory of the Amazon basin

To the north and south of the Amazon basin are some very old rocks indeed. The Brazilian and Guianan shields, as these formations are known, date from the Pre-Cambrian period, more than 600 million years ago. The rivers that drain these areas are known as clear water rivers, and the Rio Tocantins and Rio Xingu are examples. They are often blue or green in colour and very beautiful, but the water itself is clear, as the ancient rocks have been weathered over millions of years and release few minerals or nutrients into the rainwater that runs off them. These Pre-Cambrian rocks underlie the whole basin, but for most of its expanse they are buried to a great depth under layers of sediments, legacy of a vast inland sea. For, astonishingly, most scientists believe that the area we know today as the Amazon basin originally drained into the Pacific, until the rise of the Andes, a recent event in geological terms, dammed the flow and created the largest lake the world has known.

The rivers that rise in these areas of Tertiary sediments are the poorest of the Amazon rivers in terms of their nutrient load. They are also clear, but stained the colour of black coffee, a colour that appears at its most striking over the many beaches which appear in the dry season. In midstream, they appear completely black, and are known as black water rivers. The staining comes from organic acids produced by the decomposition of organic matter. The Rio Negro, the major tributary and a mighty river in its own right, fifth largest in the world, is the most famous of the black water rivers, but closer to Mamirauá, the Rio Tefé and the lake at its mouth are also black water. The chemistry of black water has an important impact on the life that it supports, not least, from the explorer's perspective, in the relief from mosquitoes along many of the black water rivers: these troublesome insects cannot breed in such acidic conditions.

Only the rivers that drain the slopes of the Andes, the youngest rocks of the basin, are known as white water rivers. This label has nothing to do with the many rapids and waterfalls as the young rivers pour down the steep slopes in Peru,

The Amazon water lily (*Victoria amazonica*), queen of the lakes, in Bolsinha Lake, a traditional walk for Mamirauá visitors.

Meeting of the waters of the Negro and Amazon rivers, near Manaus.

The waters of the Apara Channel bring new sediments from the Japurá River; this is truly a white water river. The waters of the channel of Mamirauá Lake look black because the sediments have sunk to the bottom, so here we have a false meeting of black and white waters.

Columbia and Ecuador, and everything to do with the rich sediment loads they carry from the mountains. Thrown up by a collision of the Pacific and South American plates a mere 20 million years ago, the Andes are being rapidly eroded, and the mineral salts they surrender, essential to the primary stages of life, make the water of these rivers turbid and muddy, closest in colour to frothy cocoa or *cafe au lait*. The Amazon itself, or Solimões, as the Brazilian stretch above the mouth of the Rio Negro is called, is a white water river, as is the Madeira, second in the rank of tributaries and the world's sixth largest river.

This division of the rivers by their sediment loads, chemical properties and consequent appearance is of crucial importance, not just in the geological story they tell of the origins of the basin but in understanding the subtle variations they impose on the flora and fauna that inhabit their waters and the surrounding ecosystems. The distinction is not always clear, however, and two examples from Mamirauá highlight the danger of hasty classification. The Japurá, along with the Solimões, provides one of the boundaries of the reserve, and where it joins the main river at the south-easterly tip of the protected area, appears to be a white water river. But trace its course upstream, above the town of Maraã, and it becomes clear that the Japurá is not a true white water river at all. Two branches of the Solimões, the Auati-Paraná and the Paraná do Aranapu, also important boundaries for the reserve, enter the Japurá upstream of its mouth and are responsible for its colour. The confusion can work the other way. Some of the many branches of the Amazon, as it winds across the flood plain, may at certain times of the year become cut off from the current, as we shall see. Without agitation, the sediment load drops to the bottom and the water takes on the typical colour of black water rivers, though with very different chemical and biological properties. Where true black and white waters meet, an *encontro das águas*, or meeting of the waters, is produced, one of the great natural spectacles of the Amazon. The grandest and best known example is the collision of the Rio Negro with the Solimões near to Manaus, but the Rio Tefé's entrance into the main stream, though smaller, is also impressive. The contrasting waters flow side by side downstream for several kilometres before the differences become imperceptible to the eye: even then chemical differences between water on opposite banks can be measured.

The prehistory of the Amazon basin has one more important chapter. At some stage, the land bridge separating the inland sea from the Atlantic was finally breached and the waters from the Andes began the journey they still undertake today, more than six thousand kilometres to the ocean in the east. But with the onset of the Pleistocene, about 2.5 million years ago, the earth underwent the first of a series of climactic events known as ice ages. The world became drier and much cooler, and though glaciers never rolled over the Amazon, they made their presence felt in several important ways. The enlarged ice caps trapped significant fractions of the world's water, and the sea level dropped; in the most recent of these events, some 18,000 years ago, by up to 130m. Transformed into swift streams, the Amazon and its tributaries began to carve deep gorges into the sedimentary basin across which they flowed. When the ice caps retreated, at the beginning of the present interglacial period, the Holocene, the level of the seas rose again, and the rivers backed up, creating a vast freshwater gulf. Their stately progress resumed, the white water rivers began again to deposit their heavy loads of sediment from the Andes, and a new bed of sediments was formed, and continues to be formed, within the boundaries of the ice age gorges. This is the area across which the Amazon main stream currently wanders; this is the *várzea*, or flooded forest.

The influence of the Pleistocene events is clearly seen where black and clear water streams flow into the white water Amazon. The sediment poor tributaries have been unable to fill the lakes left over from ice age erosion, and the trunk stream has partially closed off the confluence with its own rapid deposition, throwing a barrier of new *várzea* across the mouth. Behind this, the tributary is often very wide and very deep, as for example the Rio Negro at Manaus, where the river can be 14km wide and reaches depths of 100m.

Clearly the *várzea* we see today has changed radically over the millions of years of geological time. Just as surprising are the changes that occur over the passage of just one year in the flooded forest. To understand these, we must have some appreciation of the climate of the region and the extraordinary cycle of the waters of the flooded forest.

Floods and floodplains

The Andes are the major climatic discontinuity in the continent of South America. West of the mountains the land tends to be arid, with large stretches of desert, but the traveller crossing one of the high passes will notice, in just a few kilometres, major changes in the weather. The air becomes humid and the vegetation changes dramatically. Descending into the Amazon basin, our traveller is entering one of the wettest places on earth. Here, in the eastern foothills, some areas average more than 6000mm of annual rainfall. Most of this water has its origins in the Atlantic Ocean, where moisture evaporated from the surface of the ocean by the tropical sun is wafted westwards by a convergence of trade winds. Studies show that the forest cover is an efficient 'recycler' of water, returning moisture to the air via evapotranspiration. Rain falling on the upper Amazon may have fallen up to five times before, lower down the river's course.

Crucially, this rain does not fall evenly throughout the year. Though the patterns of variation are complex, due to the vast extent of the basin and its position straddling the equator, rainfall tends to be concentrated into wet seasons of intense precipitation and dry seasons when the rains are more sporadic and less intense. At

A paricarana tree (*Pythecellobium corymbosum*), in full bloom, on the shores of Mamirauá Lake.

Bird´s-eye view of the Mamirauá varzea forest where lakes that were once rivers are created by sediment deposition through the amazing dynamics of this vast floodplain.

Bird´s-eye view of the Amazon River near Mamirauá. On one bank, sediments are deposited and form beaches, but on the other side of the river, the waters erode the riverbank, and land and trees fall into the river, increasing the sediment load – a phenomenon known as *terra caída*.

Mamirauá, the season of most rain is from December to March, when three times as much rain falls as in the driest period, from July to October. Similar patterns, throughout the basin, together with the seasonal melting of the snow and ice on the high Andean peaks where some of the tributaries have their source, cause an annual variation in the amount of water carried by the main river systems. In relative terms, this variation is less significant than in other major rivers of the world: storage provided by the vast basin and the many thousands of miles separating tributaries that rise in both northern and southern hemispheres effectively 'damp' the fluctuations in rainfall. Nevertheless, such is the extent of the volumes of water in motion that at Iquitos, the major city of the Peruvian Amazon, river levels rise and fall by up to 20m each year. Further down the course of the Amazon, at Mamirauá, the flood is between 10 and 12m, though there is much variation between years. In years of high floods, virtually the whole *várzea*, up to 90km between the *terra firme* on either side of the floodplain and including the whole reserve, can be submerged. The flood 'pulse' takes about 6 months to traverse the basin, beginning in the west and moving eastward, diminishing in extent as it does so. It is this annual inundation that is the single most important factor shaping the habitat of the flooded forest and the remarkable adaptations of the flora and fauna that inhabit it.

Even at the height of the *seca* or dry season, the *várzea* is full of water, and a flight over the reserve in a small aircraft will reveal a complex mosaic of lakes, channels and cuts. During the *cheia* or flood, these are linked to a vast body of water flowing through the flooded forest; in the *seca*, however, many become completely isolated, with important implications for their biological and chemical properties. The research program has identified more than 600 of these 'lakes', and they are important resources for the inhabitants, both animal and human, of the reserve, as we shall see. One of them, Lago Mamirauá, at the heart of the Ecotourism Zone, is a tranquil stretch of water, a world away from the mighty rivers of the Solimões, several kilometres away to the west, or the Japurá, closer at hand to the east. Ten kilometres in length, it is less than 400m wide on average. Yet when Márcio Ayres began work here, in the late 1980's, he was surprised to find that his improvised depth sounder could not locate the bottom. Later sonar studies revealed the lake to be up to 46m deep, and for this reason Ayres believes that the lake was originally one of the main courses of the Amazon. Lago Mamirauá is in fact a typical ox-bow lake, the wide loop of a meander left behind when the parent stream carved a new and more direct route. This process has been crucial in shaping the *várzea* we see today: the white water rivers are in constant migration across their flood plains, eroding their banks where the current is swift and depositing suspended material where it runs more sedately. This process can be observed on any white water stream: on the outer edge of a bend the river scours the bank, undercutting the soft soils. The roots of trees are often exposed, and occasionally great sections of land fall away under the action of the water, the *terra caída* or fallen land. On the opposite bank sediments are accumulating and beaches may be visible, with pioneer species of vegetation establishing a tenuous grip on the newly formed land. This process can be dramatically fast: new, forested islands can appear in less than ten years whilst established areas, sometimes populated, may disappear over the same period. The *várzea* is a highly dynamic environment: its rivers are constantly changing their courses and with them the shape of the terrain. But as the elevation of a parcel of land changes, so does the amount of time it must spend under water in each annual flood, and the depth to which the floodwaters will cover it. These factors divide the *várzea* into several distinct ecological zones.

Chavascais and restingas

As the water begins to rise, in February and March, it breaches the banks of the lakes and channels and enters the forest. The first areas to be inundated are of course those that are lowest lying, the *chavascais*, as they are locally known. This 'land' may be submerged for eight months before the waters finally recede once more. The vegetation here tends to be sparse and low, though difficult to penetrate on foot in the brief dry season, thanks to the preponderance of thorns and vines that combine to form a forbidding thicket. Amongst the characteristic species of the *chavascal* is the munguba *Pseudobombax munguba*, from whose dark, green striped trunk the fibrous bark can be stripped to make an improvised cord. The large oval fruit, striking scarlet in colour, are a familiar sight in the months of June and July. Munguba seeds are believed to be dispersed primarily by wind. Wind dispersal is not the preferred strategy in the *várzea*, however. Instead, most trees exploit the active agents of seed dispersal that are all around them: birds, mammals, and even, here in the flooded forest, fish. Adaptations to animal dispersal often include an attractive fruit that the animal feeds on and then, having borne it unwittingly a suitable distance from the parent tree, either regurgitates or defecates the viable seed.

Another common tree of the *chavascal* is the *apuí*, or strangler fig *Ficus* spp. Mature figs are squat, massive trees, and when in fruit their branches are busy with a host of animals and birds feasting on the small green fruit filled with innumerable tiny seeds. These are ingested along with the fruit and then deposited, perhaps by a squirrel monkey or a toucan, along with their droppings in the crown of a distant tree. On germinating, the young plant sends aerial roots downwards, enmeshing the host tree in a cat's cradle of interlocking stems. In fact the fig is more properly a vine, and it is not until the roots reach the ground and the figs begins to establish its own root system that it takes on the appearance of a tree. By then the host has often died and rotted, either out competed for light by the fig or killed by the constricting action of its unwanted guest; literally strangled to death.

Chavascal during the flood season with floating vegetation.

A munguba tree (*Pseudobombax munguba*) – flower and fruits. The munguba is one of the most common trees of the *chavascal* vegetation; these lands are flooded for six to eight months of the year.

Above: the channel to Teiú Lake and low *restinga* rainforest.
Below: tachi tree on the Amazon River.

Apuí, or strangler fig, in the *chavascal*.

Bird's-eye view of the Mamirauá *varzea*: low levees covered by forest; a lake with floating vegetation (foreground), and in the background, *chavascal* vegetation and the Amazon River.

Floating meadows and *chavascal* vegetation.

As the waters continue to rise, through March and into April, they will begin to invade the lower levees, the *restinga baixa*. Levees are formed by the deposition of larger particles borne by the rivers, and are typically found lining the banks of *várzea* rivers and lakes. The *restinga baixa* may remain under water for between four to six months of the year, to depths of up to five metres. These lower levees represent a transition stage between the *chavascal* and the higher levees, and make up most of the forest cover of the *várzea*. The trees are typically taller than those of the *chavascal*, though few of the real giants of the rainforest are present. Under the canopy the going is usually easier, the undergrowth being sparse and the visibility good, though when the waters recede the ground remains sodden for several weeks before drying out thoroughly. Signature tree species of the *restinga baixa* include the matá-matá *Eschweilera albiflora*, whose seeds are protected in a cup like shell. The matá-matá relies on gravity alone to disperse its seeds: when they are ripe the cup separates and the seeds fall to the floor. The seeds do not ripen until the waters recede, in the later months of the year, but the immature seeds are heavily preyed on by birds and primates, including the uakari.

Another tree species typical of the *restinga baixa* is the piranheira *Piranhea trifoliata*. The timber of the piranheira is greatly sought after for construction, being extremely durable and resistant to the fungi that attack other woods and cause decay. The stumps of dead piranheiras, trailed with vines but refusing to rot, are a familiar sight in the reserve. This tree has also evolved formidable chemical defences for its leaves, which contain powerful toxins that make them indigestible to most folivores. The caterpillar of one species of Noctuid moth, however, has evolved the ability to digest them and attacks the trees in large numbers in August, when the young leaves appear. Fish crowd to the base of the tree to snap up any caterpillars that fall into the remaining water, amongst them some species of piranha, which may be the reason for the tree's unusual name.

In late April and May the floods begin to reach their highest levels. At last they enter the high levees, the *restinga alta*, which flood for the shortest time, only 2-4 months, and to depths of only 1-2.5m. These are the most mature of the levees, raised up by the deposition of sediments over many flood seasons, and they are home to some of the *várzea's* most magnificent trees, rivals in height to the trees of the *terra firme* forest.

One of the largest, its massive trunk covered with distinctive thorns, is the açacu *Hura crepitans*. Another tree highly resistant to the fungi that cause rot, it floats well, and this combination of properties make the açacu the first choice for the huge *bóias* or floats, on which the floating houses typical of the *várzea* are constructed. Açacu floats can last thirty years in the water before they need to be replaced. They are floated out from the forest during the wet season. But in the preceding dry season the bark is cut to 'bleed' the tree of the sap, which is highly toxic and can cause blindness. A traditional method of fishing uses this sap to incapacitate fish,

Low *restinga* vegetation in the dry and the flood seasons. The undergrowth is very sparse and the mean basal area of the trees is lower than that of the high *restinga*. Above, the fruit of matamatá, favoured by the uakari. Below, fruits of the piranheira tree and the tree itself, with its roots submerged.

which can then be easily harvested, but this is now banned within the reserve. The local name of the tree refers to the unfortunate after-effects of careless use of the leaves in jungle hygiene!

Perhaps the most distinctive tree of the whole *várzea* is found in the *restinga alta*. The samaumeira *Ceiba pentandra* is an emergent species: in mature trees the trunk, massively buttressed, bursts through the rest of the canopy before diverging in a crown of branches which can extend thirty metres out over the lesser trees below. Samaumeiras are the great landmarks of the flooded forest, each graceful dome being visible from far off. The English name for this tree is the Kapok or Silk-cotton, after the cotton like material in which the seeds are wrapped. Unusually for *várzea* trees, the seeds mature at the time of low water, when the samaumeira also sheds its leaves. Along with its elevated position, this adaptation allows the wind free passage through the tree, and the kapok balls with their cargo of seed are dispersed on the breeze through the forest.

As the river borne sediments continue to build them up, the high levees may reach an elevation at which they only flood in years of exceptionally high water. They are on their way to becoming *terra firme* forest. But elsewhere the river is busy creating new channels, lakes, and *chavascais*, and so the processes of destruction and construction go on.

Each hectare of Mamirauá *várzea* supports between 80 and 120 different species of tree. In a temperate forest, you might find two or three in the same area. Yet the figure in some of the *terra firme* forests of the western Amazon can approach 300. The *várzeas* of the white water floodplains, and the *igapós*, as the equivalent areas along the black water rivers are known, do not sustain such high levels of biodiversity as the *terra firme* forests that surround them. Only a limited set of species have undergone the particular adaptations required by the unique challenge of a half submerged life. What these specific adaptations are, however, is in many cases still unknown. Only a few of the *várzea* trees, for example, use aerial roots to gain access to oxygen during the period when their conventional root structure is underwater. Yet more than two or three metres beneath the surface the water in the flooded forest contains virtually no oxygen, and what little is present is largely taken up in the process of decomposition. How do the species without aerial roots survive? And how do the young seedlings and saplings cope during the early years of their life, when they may emerge from the water for only a few short weeks before being submerged once more? Despite intensive research, we simply don't yet know the answer. It's one of the continuing mysteries of the unique world of the flooded forest.

High *restinga* vegetation in the dry season on the shores of Mamirauá Lake. These levees lie underwater for only three or four months of the year, during the most severe floods, which allows the trees to grow taller, with thicker trunks.

Huge buttress roots of the kapok tree (*Ceiba pentandra*) in high *restinga* vegetation.
The *Aechmea beeriana* bromeliad.

Top: a *Heliconia marginata* inflorescence, and fruits of the marajá palm (*Bactris* sp.).

An aquatic garden with aninga arums (*Montrichardia arborescens*) and water hyacinths (*Eichhornia crassipes*).

A floating *Neptunia* sp.

Orchid (left); flower of the mungubarana tree (*Pachira aquatica*), and the edible fruits of camu-camu (*Myrciaria dubia*), extremely rich in vitamin C.

False rice (*Oryza rufipogon*) and the flower of a plant from the Myrtaceae family.

RIBEIRINHOS: THE PEOPLE OF THE VÁRZEA

Even for the flooded forest, 1999 was an exceptional year. The last flood of the old century brought its second highest water levels, and in the *terra firme* town of Tefé a foot of Amazon water flowed across the dance floor of the Tropical nightclub. In the *várzea* proper, in the remote communities of Mamirauá, things were much more serious. The small wooden houses here are raised high up on stilts for just this eventuality, but even so the river poured in through the windows of many before it finally stopped rising, and the wakes of passing boats came washing through the living rooms. But despite their perilous position, more than twenty miles in some cases from the nearest piece of solid land, there was no sense of disaster or talk of mass evacuation in the communities. Some people moved in with friends or relatives living on higher ground, abandoning their houses to the river until falling water levels allowed them back to begin the task of cleaning up. But most simply stayed put and lifted themselves clear of the floods by raising the planks of their floors. There in tiny spaces under their roofs, whole families and their few possessions waited out the floods. The fortunate or far-sighted had built floating houses secured to buoys made from the trunks of *várzea* trees: their main concern was to avoid running aground when the water finally receded. Cattle huddled on floating corrals, munching grass cut from floating meadows. Even the dogs had floating kennels. Like the other inhabitants of the *várzea* described in this book, the people of Mamirauá have learned to live with the rise and fall of the waters, and its profound impact on all aspects of their economy and culture. So completely is their way of life bound up with the river that they call themselves the *ribeirinhos*, the river people.

A fluid past

The majority of the *ribeirinhos* resident in Mamirauá today trace their ancestry to the mixing of Amerindian and European peoples following the arrival of the first Portuguese settlers in the sixteenth and seventeenth centuries. But the *várzea* supported substantial human populations long before that. Archaeological evidence sug-

The river people are a nice blend of Amazon Indian and migrants from Brazil's dry northeastern region. These beautiful, joyful people are amazingly well adapted to the harsh conditions of the flooded forest.

During severe floods, like those of 1993, the river people raise the floors of their houses to escape the floodwaters. Note the beds and the children near the roof (upper); since the floor was raised, the door cannot be opened, and the people must come and go out of the windows instead (lower).

Upper: At high water, a floating garden of green onions for flavoring fish.
Lower: as the pastures are flooded, the cattle are confined to rafts and the river people feed them on grass cut from the floating meadows.

Boca do Mamirauá in the dry and the flood seasons. Notice the water level on the bank in front of the settlement.

gests that settled groups of people were harvesting the abundant resources of fish and shellfish along the white water rivers as much as eight thousand years ago. These early *várzea* settlers were the first people in the New World to develop the skills of pottery making, and by three thousand years before the present they were supplementing their fish diet with the cultivation of manioc on the fertile soils of the floodplain. Man's adaptations to the special demands of life in the flooded forest, and his impacts in exploiting and managing that unique environment, are millennia old.

But the dynamic nature of the *várzea* environment means that individual settlements can rarely claim a long history. The constant migrations of the rivers across their flood plains simultaneously threaten some areas with erosion or *'terra caída'*, whilst isolating others behind vast beaches of deposited silt from their vital water supplies. Few of the present day communities of Mamirauá have been in their current locations for more than a couple of generations. Barroso in the northern section of the reserve has occupied three different sites since its establishment as a community sixty years ago. Nearer to the Ecotourism Zone, Boca do Mamirauá lay abandoned for fifteen years until it was reoccupied in 1987.

Older Boca residents recall *ribeirinho* families on the present site as long ago as the 1930's, but as with many Mamirauá communities, a dominant role in its history was played by a *patrão*, or patron. From his strategic stronghold at the mouth of the rich and productive Mamirauá lake system, this powerful trader ran the area as his personal fiefdom, allowing entry to the fishing grounds only to those *ribeirinhos* who sold their catch to him and purchased goods from his store. Trespassers could expect the *patrão* to empty his shotgun at their canoe. It was a lucrative monopoly. At its height in the 1940's, a visitor might have seen ten or more boats tied up waiting to be loaded with pirarucu fish and caiman skin. The two *sapucaia* trees that are such landmarks of the village today date from this period. But health problems eventually forced the return of the *patrão* to his native Northeast, and the families living in the area dispersed. The return of *ribeirinhos* to the Boca in 1987 was followed by the construction of a school in 1988, and today the community is thriving. For many families, incomes from fishing and farming are supplemented by the wages of community members, both from Boca and other nearby settlements, who work as guides and helpers at the Ecotourism lodge.

The vazante

The retreat of the floodwater is called the *vazante*, or 'emptying', and signals the start of the agricultural year in the *várzea*. Manioc is the staple of the Mamirauá communities: as *farinha* or flour it is eaten at every meal and no meal is complete without it. As the fields or *roças* are exposed in July and August, manioc planting can begin, using cuttings or *'maniva'* taken from last year's plants. If the flood has been especially heavy, people may have to borrow cuttings from neighbours or from other communities. Plot size varies widely, but most families will have at least a small *roça* or garden. Manioc is a hardy crop, resistant to drought and the many pests and diseases present in the *várzea* environment. Even so, families go to the *roça* to weed and tend the growing plants at regular intervals.

By September the water is dropping rapidly, and huge quantities of fish are becoming trapped in the *várzea* lakes. This is the time of highest productivity for the *ribeirinho* fishermen. Fishing goes on year round in Mamirauá to provide a protein component to the daily diet, but the months of falling and low water levels represent the best chance for families to supplement their income by catching fish to sell. The prize species that have traditionally earned the highest prices in the markets of Tefé and Manaus are the *pirarucu* and the *tambaqui*, but other fish that find a ready market are the *tucunaré* or peacock bass and various species of *peixe liso* or catfish.

Whilst men and women share in the work on the *roça*, fishing is usually, though not exclusively, a male activity. Some of the best fishing can be in hidden lakes some distance from the communities, through the confusing maze of channels and cuts. Fishing trips often last several days, and groups of men and boys will leave to camp in the forest in a convoy of canoes piled with ice chests and enough *farinha* to sustain them until their return. *Ribeirinhos* are expert fishermen and employ a baffling range of techniques. Various types of nets, traps, rods and lines and harpoons are all employed, depending on the season and the species. Maintaining equipment is a major task, with the damage inflicted by piranha attacks on nets a particular problem.

The problem of fishing to sell, rather than simply to provide a meal for the family, is the speed at which even the freshest fish will spoil in the hot and humid climate. Ice is expensive and difficult to obtain, and the *ribeirinho* must dispose of his catch quickly if he is to realise any return on his investment of time and effort. Traditionally, this has meant either a long and expensive journey to market in the towns of Tefé or Alvarães, or selling the fish to itinerant traders known as *regatões*, who pass through the communities selling basic groceries and buying fish. It's a buyer's market, however, and the price on offer is often very poor. To fill this gap, one of the Mamirauá communities is experimenting with an innovative cooperative marketing project.

The seca

October and November are high summer in the *várzea*. During the seca or dry season, the weather is at its hottest, with clear skies and a broiling sun, and the *ribeirinhos* may have to trek long distances across the wide beaches to fetch water or to wash dishes. Traditionally, drinking water came from the river, though

Children learn early on how to handle the fishing tools they will use as adults to make a living.
Fishermen: aruanãs and bodós caught in the fishnets.

The process of peeling and roasting manioc to make flour is the river people's main activity at the outset of the flood season. The canoe is used to hold the peeled manioc, and the paddle as a shovel to stir the flour as it roasts.

Traditional clay pots are handcrafted mainly by the women who have found a promising source of income from ecotourism.

many families now collect rainwater as a healthier alternative. With this year's manioc crop still some months from harvest, and last year's supplies running low, some families may need to buy or borrow from neighbours to get by. But other crops supplement the diet at this time of the year, such as the *melancia* or watermelon, widely grown and enjoyed in Mamirauá.

The football pitch occupies pride of place in many communities, and with the floodwaters gone and the pitch dried out the season can begin. Football is no less of an obsession in Mamirauá than in the rest of Brazil, and the whole community is involved on the day of a big match, with both women's and men's teams competing and the less athletic turning out to pass judgement on the merits of the performance. Games are always passionately contested and almost invariably followed by a knees-up before the visiting team and their supporters depart by boat. The arrival of satellite TV means that some communities can now follow the fortunes of the national league clubs, and on match days the school or church is packed with rival supporters watching the game on the village set.

The enchente

The heavy rains that often set in after Christmas signify the end of the *várzea* summer and the beginning of a dilemma for the farmers that becomes more and more acute as the floodwaters rise once again. The *enchente* or 'filling' is the harvest season, and it is imperative that the manioc tubers are removed before the *roças* flood and the crop is spoiled. But pull them too soon and the yield will be small as valuable growing time is lost. The *ribeirinhos* must calculate, consult their own and their neighbours store of knowledge about the river's fickle behaviour, and eventually take a gamble one way or the other. The river does not help: it will rise steadily for a week only to fall again, a confusing phenomenon known as a *repiquete*. Nothing is predictable. By March, however, most people have an opinion as to how fast and how far the river will flood, and within a few weeks the manioc harvest is in full swing.

This is the busiest time of year for the *ribeirinho* family, and everybody helps out. The complicated process of processing manioc remains essentially the same as that followed by the Indians when the first European settlers arrived. Manioc is a root crop, and whilst a sweet variety can be eaten straight from the ground (called *macaxeira* and made into delicious chips), most of the crop is actually poisonous in its raw state. Part of the success with which it resists pest attack is due to the presence in the tubers of hydrocyanic acid, or cyanide. To remove this unwelcome ingredient, the tubers are first soaked in a canoe until they ferment and soften, and then peeled and grated into a mash. The mash is drained of the noxious juice by squeezing in a palm fibre tube known as a *tipití*, and then sieved and toasted on a huge griddle, whilst being diligently stirred using a wooden paddle. The end product is *farinha*: hard and crunchy granules more like yellow Grape nuts than flour. The by-products of the process are not wasted. The clear portion of the extracted liquid is used to make a distinctive sauce called *tucupí*, whilst the solids that separate out provide *tapioca*, a sweeter flour used to make *beiju* pancakes and biscuits.

The cheia

With the manioc successfully harvested, the *ribeirinhos* wait to see how high the flood water will rise, and if they will need to raise their floors or even, in exceptional years, evacuate to stay with family in nearby communities or in the towns, to wait out the floods. Mostly, though, the people of Mamirauá remain throughout the *cheia*, or high water season, and make the best of a life lived almost entirely by canoe. Those needing timber to repair or improve their houses take advantage of the entry of the water into the *restingas* to fell selected trees and float them out. Timber cutting can also be a source of income during the *cheia* when fishing is poor, and Mamirauá staff are working with some communities to draw up sustainable plans that will allow them to harvest commercial timber legally. Fishing is poor during the *cheia*, but wild game makes a more frequent appearance in the *ribeirinho* pot. Howler monkey and *jabuti* tortoise are both relished.

Otherwise, with both fields and football pitch underwater, there is not much to do. Fishermen spend long periods mending nets, and there is much visiting of neighbours and relatives. A feature of many of these get-togethers is the production and consumption of *açai*. The *açaizeiro* is a graceful palm tree that around this time of year produces a crop of small, hard fruit. These are soaked and crushed in a canoe in much the way that grapes were once trodden in France, and in the same way everyone gets cheerfully covered in thick purplish liquor. *Açai* is non-alcoholic, but nonetheless seems to have a soporific quality, and after several rounds of the brew thickened with *farinha*, everybody heads for the hammock. *Ribeirinho* children, of course, always find plenty to do, and lead a semi-aquatic life leaping in and out of the water swirling around the houses. For young children there is an obvious danger, and parents have to keep an eye on the toddlers.

Of course, *ribeirinho* families face more pressing problems than boredom in the long weeks of the *cheia*. Access to health facilities is very limited, and problems linked to poor sanitation, such as intestinal parasites and diarrhoea, are not uncommon, especially among children. Without proper treatment, these can be life threatening, and a third of mothers will have lost a child before its fifth birthday. In general, however, the abundance of the *várzea* and its rivers means that illnesses related to poor nutrition are less common in the *várzea* than in other rural areas of the developing world, though the *ribeirinho* sweet tooth means that tooth decay is widespread (up to a kilo of sugar a day may be consumed in some households).

Most of the larger communities now contain a school, but these are seldom able

During the flood season, children play in the water, with no thought of stingrays or piranhas, while adults mend their fishnets and collect fruits from the assai palm to make a delicious beverage.

School in a *varzea* settlement.

Fish and manioc flower, a typical noonday meal menu in the *varzea*. Shown here in the traditional way the people eat their meals.

Grilled fish is a typical dish served at community gatherings during religious festivals or weekend soccer tournaments.

to provide more than a basic primary education, and young people wanting to continue their education often have to move to the towns and live with relatives while they attend school. On the other hand, many children may not attend school at all, or attend sporadically, needed instead by their parents to work. The support and services that communities receive from municipal government vary widely depending on which administrative region they fall into. Many *ribeirinhos* are critical of politicians who visit rural areas only during election campaigns. A tradition of exchanging gifts for votes persists in some areas.

The festa

But once a year such problems are set aside as the community celebrates the festival of its patron saint. These *festas* last for up to ten days, and involve not just the members of the celebrating community but people from a wide area who come to join the party. Festivities begin with the raising of the mast, a pole cut from the forest nearby and decorated with leaves and fruit. After prayers for the saint and a procession of the image, the mast is erected with a great barrage of firecrackers, and the *festa* has begun. A communal meal is provided, and copious quantities of beer and *cachaça*, a potent sugar cane liquor, are consumed. The *festa* plays a crucial social function in these remote communities, bringing together separated relatives and providing a chance for the resolution of disputes or the hatching of new plans. In these rare opportunities to meet people from outside the immediate area lie the origins of many *ribeirinho* marriages. Before long a *forró*, the seductive dance rhythm originally from the Northeast but hugely popular throughout Amazonia, will be playing, and the dancing will begin.

ARBOREAL MAMMALS

Crashing through the canopy, setting the treetops shaking, a leaping form clears the gap between two branches high above the trail. Inquisitive eyes peer down at the intruders and a curious chirruping conversation follows. A close encounter with an arboreal mammal is the highlight of many visits to Mamirauá, and tree dwelling mammals are well adapted to life in the *várzea*. But though the annual inundation does not deprive them of their habitat, as is the case with terrestrial animals, it has shaped their development as species. Primates in particular will always be associated with Mamirauá, because of the role that primate research played in the establishment of the reserve, already discussed earlier in this book. The Ecotourism Zone at Mamirauá has four species of primate, fewer than neighbouring areas of *terra firme* forest. Two of the species are however endemic to Mamirauá: their entire known range is within the boundaries of the reserve. It seems likely that the broad rivers forming these boundaries and the annual *várzea* flood have been important factors in isolating these populations. In more distant and elevated areas of the reserve, up to three other species of primate, more typical of the *terra firme* arboreal fauna, also occur. Their presence may indicate areas of transition between the *várzea* and *terra firme* ecosystems.

New World primates differ from their Old World counterparts, including man, in the orientation of their nostrils, and in the development by some species of a prehensile tail, the ability to use the tail as a fifth limb, particularly when moving through or feeding in the high canopy. There is some dispute as to the origin of the Neotropical primates, but most of the evidence now seems to suggest that they crossed over to the continent of South America from Africa, rather than from North America. The pedigree of the other main group of arboreal mammals is very distinguished indeed: the sloths and anteaters represent some of the last living members of a family of mammals that came into existence with the first major explosion in mammal diversity in South America, in the Paleocene period more than 50 million years ago.

The white uakari (*Cacajao calvus calvus*), still on the endangered species list, is an effective seedeater that lives in the canopy of the tallest trees at Mamirauá. Its entire range is protected by the Mamirauá Sustainable Development Reserve.

The White Uakari

In 1855, in the unlikely surroundings of the port of Tefé, Bates described his first encounter with a monkey of a 'most grotesque appearance. Their bodies (about eighteen inches in height, exclusive of limbs) were clothed from neck to tail with very long, straight and shining whitish hair; their heads were nearly bald...and their faces glowed with the most vivid scarlet hue.' The unfortunate animals were on their way to Rio de Janeiro, as presents for a high ranking government official, and had been obtained 'with great difficulty in the forests which cover the lowlands, near the principal mouth of the Japurá...'

Bates knew that the white uakari *Cacajao calvus calvus* was unique to the forests near to Tefé, but he had no idea quite how restricted its range would turn out to be. Later research has shown that the monkey is found only in the *várzea* floodplain between the Japurá and Solimões rivers and the Auati-Paraná Canal, exactly the boundaries that today define the Mamirauá reserve. This is no accident: as is described earlier in this book, the reserve was first created as an immediate consequence of Márcio Ayres pioneering research, to protect these extraordinary animals.

Quite why the white uakari is so confined we do not know: whether this is a refuge from competition with other species, or whether the species has only recently evolved and not yet had time to disperse to other areas is unclear. Two other related species replace *Cacajao calvus calvus* in adjoining regions, however: further west we find the red uakari *C. calvus rubicundus*, and in the *igapó* forest along the black water rivers to the east is the black uakari *C. melanocephalus*.

All the uakaris are flooded forest specialists, and they have adapted to exploit an astonishing variety of the food resources of their habitat. In one and a half years observing uakari near the Ecotourism Zone in Mamirauá, Ayres recorded their use of more than a hundred separate tree species in their foraging. Fruit is the uakari's favourite food, but the *várzea* trees tend to come into fruit at the same season. To cope with this seasonal imbalance in the availability of their preferred diet, uakari eat large quantities of seeds and immature fruits. Their powerful teeth are able to crack open even the toughest husks and shells to crush the seeds within them, and uakaris, along with macaws and parrots, are formidable seed predators of the flooded forest.

Their diet is supplemented in a number of other enterprising ways. In August, when moth caterpillars emerge to attack the new leaves of the piranheira tree, the uakaris congregate in these trees and feast on them. The leaves are toxic but the caterpillars are not, and so the monkeys exploit a food resource that would otherwise be unavailable to them. At the same time, they enjoy a nutritional windfall: the grubs contain twice the protein and three times the fat of the leaves on which they feed.

Later still in the year, when the water levels have fallen to their lowest and the shoots of new plants are appearing in the now dry forest floor, uakari will sometimes descend from the trees to browse on the ground, uprooting the new shoots to get at the nutrients still contained in the germinating seed beneath.

The high energetic content of its diet makes the uakari the most active primate for its weight in the world. In the fruiting seasons, groups of monkeys made up of between 25 and 50 individuals can travel more than 5 kilometres during a day. They are agile monkeys, using their short and stumpy tails to brace and balance, and can leap gaps of twenty metres or more between trees. Living over water for much of the year, they can also swim, though always reluctantly. The uakari's curious name may come from its most common vocalisation, a low-pitched 'Ka-ka-ka' made whilst the animal is feeding or resting.

Squirrel and Capuchin Monkeys

Though now protected throughout their range, uakari are still relatively rare and quite shy, and careful tracking is usually required to find a group in the wild. Much more common, and so curious that they will often find the visitor rather than the other way around, are two primates which are often found together, the squirrel monkey *Saimiri* spp. and the brown capuchin monkey *Cebus apella*. Both of these monkeys are omnivores *par excellence*, and supplement a diet of fruit with nectar, seeds, molluscs, small vertebrates and eggs, when the opportunity presents itself. Both species spend up to half of their time hunting for insects with which to add protein to their diets. The capuchins forage destructively, noisily tearing up dead and hollow branches and rustling through debris in tree crowns and vine tangles, looking for ants and termites. Squirrel monkeys meanwhile turn over leaf litter and take insects flushed by other canopy predators such as the Greater Ani *Crotophaga major*, sometimes leaping with great agility to take them on the wing.

The capuchins may well be the most intelligent of the New World monkeys, and their social interactions are complex, with a great variety of vocalisations especially as the group of 20-30 individuals spreads out to feed. Though lacking the specialised dentition of the uakari, they will bash hard-shelled fruit against the trunks of trees to break them, and use twigs to extract insects from inaccessible crevices. Unlike the uakari or the squirrel monkey, the capuchin has the beginnings of a prehensile tail, though this is nothing like the sophisticated fifth limb of the howler monkeys, for example. But the capuchin makes up for this with great manual dexterity. Their curiosity is second to none, and they are often implicated in the theft of the brightly coloured labels that Mamirauá researchers have painstakingly affixed to trees in their study areas.

The squirrel monkey is by far the most numerous of the Mamirauá primates, and moves in large bands of up to 50 individuals or more, which roam over extensive

There are two species of squirrel monkey at Mamirauá. The black squirrel monkey (*Saimiri vanzolinii*) is endemic to Mamirauá, while the common squirrel monkey (*Saimiri sciureus*) is widespread in the Brazilian Amazon. The black squirrel monkey is the most commonly seen primate species in the Ecotourism Zone.the Mamirauá Sustainable Development Reserve.

The brown capuchin monkey (*Cebus apella*) forages at all levels of the Mamirauá forest. It can sometimes be seen gathering fallen fruits, insects or small vertebrates on the ground.

areas of more than 50 hectares. The arrival of the group is often signalled by a chorus of high pitched, bird like chirruping and whistling. The territory of a band of *Saimiri* may include several bands of the less mobile *Cebus*, and the squirrel monkeys seem to use the capuchins as guides to fruiting trees in their smaller and thus better patrolled home ranges. They will not hesitate to drop the association with one band of *Cebus* and take up with another should the supply of fruiting trees begin to dry up.

As recently as 1985, a new species of squirrel monkey was identified in the area of the reserve to the east of the community of Jarauá. *Saimiri vanzolinii* is very similar to its more widespread cousin, *Saimiri sciureus*, but can be distinguished by its blackish head and by the black line that runs from the crown to the tip of the tail. The total range of the blackish squirrel monkey is believed to be only about 950 square kilometres: thus Mamirauá is distinguished not just by the presence of two wholly endemic species of monkey but by the fact that one of them has the smallest range of any neotropical primate.

Howlers

A strong farmyard smell on a trail through the Mamirauá *várzea* forest will often precede the discovery of large piles of droppings like yellow ping-pong balls. This marks the spot where, high in the canopy overhead, a troop of red howler monkeys *Alouatta seniculus* have spent the night. They may still be close by, and if they take fright the visitor may be treated to one of the more bizarre *várzea* experiences, as the alarmed monkeys position themselves overhead and let fly with a indignant barrage of urine and fragrant dung! As the whiff suggests, howlers are herbivores, and whilst they will eat fruit when it is available, they are unique amongst New World monkeys in their adaptations to a diet of leaves.

The tropical rainforest is a leafy place. Estimates of the production of a hectare of forest vary between five and eighteen tonnes of new leaves every year, depending on the nature of the forest and the methodology used. Clearly this represents an abundant resource for an animal capable of exploiting it. But rainforest plants can ill afford to surrender all their leaves to hungry herbivores, and have evolved a whole suite of defensive weapons to deter leaf predators. These include physical deterrents such as sharp thorns or spines, active patrolling by stinging ants or wasps who make their home in the plant, and a range of chemical weapons known as secondary compounds that have various toxic effects. Still more problematical for the would-be folivore is a simple carbohydrate called cellulose, which forms the main constituent of plant cell walls, and which the digestive systems of most vertebrates cannot break down.

To get around this problem, most leaf eating animals recruit a colony of symbiotic bacteria, microbe enzymes that break down the cellulose as it passes through the gut. This process of fermentation is usually housed in an extended gut system, and in the howlers it takes place towards the end of the animal's digestion in a specially enlarged colon and caecum. This is only partly effective, as there is then little time for the nutrients to be absorbed. In any event, a diet of fermented leaves is low in energy, and the howlers lead a very different life to the hyperactive squirrel and capuchin monkeys. They have a relatively low metabolic rate, and spend more than three-quarters of the day in rest, allowing the slow process of leaf digestion to run its course.

The home range of a troop of howlers is consequently compact, only about 8-12 ha in Mamirauá, and they tend to favour the *restinga alta* or high levees, where they spend most of their time in the higher branches of the large trees, rarely descending to the understory, where thin saplings and brush might not bear their weight. Howlers are the finest *várzea* exponents of the prehensile tail, which is tipped with a pad of bare skin like a palm, and which they make much use of as a fifth limb, when moving through the forest or to anchor themselves to a branch when feeding or sleeping.

In the *várzea* howler troops are relatively small, made up of about 6 animals with one or sometimes two dominant males. The males are about 30% larger than the females, and will expel or even kill young males in the group who threaten their dominance. In contrast, confrontations between groups are rare, thanks to the potent communication tool that is also one of the *várzea's* most evocative sounds: the howl of the howler monkey.

Visitors rising early on their first day in Mamirauá are often greeted by a reverberating roar that rolls around the forest and seems to come from all directions at once. The local troop of howler monkeys are up and about, and are letting neighbouring troops (and tourists) know exactly where they are so that any unwanted intrusions can be avoided. With all those leaves to digest, howlers cannot afford the time to patrol their boundaries and confront rival bands face to face. Instead they howl, a much more efficient brand of diplomacy. The hyroid bone at the base of the tongue is greatly enlarged, and air is passed over a hole in it rather like blowing across the neck of a bottle. Howling is common at dawn and dusk, and during heavy rain, and heard up to several kilometres away it is one of the unforgettable experiences of the flooded forest.

At the very end of the dry season, the fruiting of the many fig trees *Ficus* spp. offers a rare opportunity to observe all four of the Mamirauá primates in close proximity. The fruits provide a sudden abundance at a time when other food is scarce, and the sight of all four monkeys calmly feeding in the same tree is an illustration of the importance of figs to many *várzea* species, and of how quite different ecological niches may overlap under certain conditions.

The brown-throated three-toed sloth (*Bradypus variegatus*), at left, and the red howler monkey (*Alouatta seniculus*) are the most common leaf-eating arboreal mammals of Mamirauá.

The Amazon red squirrel (*Sciurus* spp.).

The coati *Nasua nasua* is not exclusively arboreal, but feels at ease to move in the tree canopies.

Sloths

Another group of mammals have adopted the leaf eating life, and been so successful that they make up the single largest component of the *várzea* mammal biomass. But you would hardly know it: though they are common, you need sharp eyes to spot the Brown-throated three-toed sloth *Bradypus variegatus* in the trees along the water's edge. Sloths are highly cryptic, cultivating a crop of green algae in microscopic grooves in their hair as further camouflage. And they keep very, very still. A sloth is so completely adapted to its low energy leaf diet that its metabolic rate is some 25% below normal for its weight. 80% of the sloth day is spent in rest, and movement, when it comes, is so ponderous as to be almost comic. They can in fact move quite well between the forty or so trees that make up their home range, though on the ground they are relatively helpless. Sloths are good if slow swimmers, and have even been sighted crossing the Amazon itself. But it takes them a very long time to reach the other side.

Sloths hang upside down from their favoured trees using long claws on their feet. Unlike most mammals, their fur grows from the belly towards the back, an adaptation to this topsy-turvy life that helps rain to run off the animal more easily. *Ficus* and *Cecropia* trees are particular favourites, and they seem to prefer the low lying *chavascais*, though they are found in numbers in the other *várzea* habitats. Sloths are solitary, and the only significant bond seems to be between mother and young, which lasts for about six months, in which time the young sloth is introduced to the important food trees in the area.

One of the trees in the sloth's range is singled out for a very particular honour. At any moment, up to a third of a sloth's weight may be made up of fermenting leaves. Like everything else, sloth digestion is not rapid: it may take 250 hours for breakfast to work its way through the large and complex gut system. But roughly once a week, the sloth makes its way deliberately to the base of one particular tree in its territory, and there on the ground defecates neatly before beginning its slow climb back up into the canopy. In Mamirauá, several animals have been observed using the same tree for this purpose. The reason for this extraordinary behaviour has been the cause of much speculation. Are the sloths marking territory? Or composting a favourite tree? Whatever the reason it must be a very good one for the sloth, who incurs such effort and danger in his weekly pilgrimage.

Another curious aspect of sloth life is that their body clocks seem to be awry. Observing sloths on the banks of Lago Mamirauá, Helder Queiroz, a researcher at the Mamirauá project, noticed that the circadian cycle, or daily rhythm, of the animal seemed not to be synchronised with the 24 hour solar cycle, like the vast majority of animals including ourselves, but rather last for about 27 hours. Active periods for the sloths under observation changed gradually from day to day. Queiroz suggested that this might allow sloths to make even more use of limited areas, as effectively the animals in a section of forest have spread themselves out not just in space but in time as well.

Sloths are amongst the survivors of an ancient and very important group of South American mammals. The Edentata (sometimes called Xenartha) emerged at the end of the Paleocene, after South America had split from the other landmasses that made up Gondwanaland. From fossil evidence, scientists now believe that in the consequent isolation four families of sloth-like mammals emerged, including tree dwellers and terrestrial animals, some of which were four-ton giants. The arrival of the North American mammals, in the event known as the Great Faunal Interchange that followed the rise of the isthmus at Panama, led to the extinction of almost all of these animals. Only *Bradypus* and the rare and nocturnal two-toed sloth *Choloepus* spp. remain.

Other arboreal mammals

Another member of the Edentata occasionally seen in Mamirauá is the collared anteater *Tamandua tetradactyla*. As the name suggests, these distinctive animals feed mainly on ants, termites and bees, and can often be located by following the sounds of tearing wood, as the anteater rips apart the nests of its prey. The tubular snout contains no teeth but an extendable tongue covered with sticky saliva that makes an excellent instrument for lapping up insects. Aside from their noisy foraging, anteaters are largely silent, unlike another distinctive inhabitant of the *várzea* trees, the Amazon bamboo rat *Dactylomys dactylinus*. Nocturnal and diminutive, they are rarely seen but often heard, especially about an hour after sunset. The distinctive call, a staccato *coró-coró*, gives the rat its local name, and is often mistakenly attributed to a frog.

Two other residents of the *várzea* canopy that visitors stand a good chance of seeing are the Amazon red squirrel *Sciurus* spp. and the coati *Nasua nasua*. The latter, a member of the racoon family, is not strictly arboreal, being equally at home foraging on the forest floor for invertebrates as feeding on fruit in the high branches. Rusty red in colour with a long snout, the coati's most distinctive feature is the long banded tail, which is usually held vertically and often gives away the animal's progress through the undergrowth. *Sciurus* is a large, coppery red squirrel with a conspicuous bushy tail, and flexible ankle joints that give it the useful ability to walk head first down tree trunks. Preferred food includes fruit and the hard shelled seeds of some palm trees, which like its temperate relatives the Amazon squirrel often stores in caches against lean times.

OTHER MAMMALS

The herbivorous terrestrial fauna of the *terra firme* forest, species such as tapir, peccary and brocket deer, are not generally found in the seasonally inundated *várzea*, though they may be opportunistic visitors during the dry season, especially to the more elevated areas of the reserve. Their ecological role in releasing the nutrients available in plant materials is taken on here by animals at home in the water, good swimmers such as the capybara, and by one of the group of mammals to have adopted an entirely aquatic lifestyle, the Amazon manatee.

Manatee

Manatees belong to the order Sirenia, named after the mermaids of classical mythology, though it is hard to imagine even the loneliest of sailors being seduced by the *peixe-boi*, or fish-ox, as the animal is known throughout Amazonia. Shaped like a fat cigar, with a single flat paddle for a tail and a bristly moustache on the upper lip; unlike the mermaid the song of the manatee is only audible under water. From above only the occasional puff might be heard as the nostrils break surface and the manatee breathes. The Amazon manatee *Trichechus inunguis* is the smallest of the world's manatees, but even so a large adult may reach 500kg, making the *peixe-boi* the largest living inhabitant of the South American continent.

The manatee's food resources are the huge quantities of floating grasses, water hyacinth, water lettuce and sedge that flourish along the margins of the *várzea* lakes and channels during the period of high water. Non-ruminants, manatees ferment this plant material in their hindguts, a relatively inefficient process that means they must be voracious grazers. An adult manatee can eat up to 50kg of floating vegetation a day, some 50% of which is returned to the water in characteristic

The largest rodent in the world, the capybara – one meter long on an average, up to 50cm tall at the shoulder and weighing about 60kg. It is not common at Mamirauá, but with luck, visitors may get a glimpse of this amazing mammal.

Besides the jaguar and the puma, the margay cat (*Felis wiedii*) is also found at Mamirauá. It feeds on small vertebrates on the forest floor or in trees, where it climbs with incredible agility.

The Amazonian manatee (*Trichechus inunguis*) is South America's largest and heaviest freshwater mammal. It is a harmless, docile animal, but shy and hard to find in the wild. It feeds exclusively on water plants.

horse-like droppings which float to the surface. This mass of organic fertiliser is exploited by a whole community of fish, crustaceans and plankton who could otherwise make no use of the huge weight of vegetable matter floating by overhead.

Mamirauá means 'baby manatee' in the indigenous tupi language, and researchers now believe that the lakes around the Ecotourism zone are important for manatee reproduction. Birth takes place towards the start of the flood season, to ensure a plentiful supply of food. Manatees build up large reserves of fat during this period, because when the water levels drop they must abandon the *várzea* lakes for the river channels and deeper lakes, where the availability of food is much reduced. Radio tracking of the manatees that come to Mamirauá during the floods to feed shows that they migrate, as the water level falls, to Lago Amanã, a black water lake in the *terra firme* of the neighbouring Amanã reserve, to wait out the dry season. The manatees of Mamirauá thus depend on both ecosystems for their survival.

Manatees have poor eyesight but seem to find their way in the dark world under the floating meadows using taste buds on the tongue. Their size and thick hide mean they have no natural predators. But they have been hunted by man for centuries, using a harpoon to bring the animal to the bank and then wooden plugs driven into the nostrils to suffocate it. Bates describes the meat and fat as having 'somewhat the taste of very coarse pork…of a disagreeably fishy flavour.' More recently manatees were persecuted for their hide, which for a brief period in the middle of the twentieth century was much in demand for industrial belting and gaskets. Although large herds were once common, the *peixe-boi* is today endangered throughout its range, and is still under heavy hunting pressure despite legal protection and a vigorous campaign of public education. Their best defence against man is a sharp sense of hearing and the ability to remain submerged for long periods of time when danger threatens. Manatees have a metabolic rate more than 50% lower than normal for animals of their size, and can stay underwater for up to an hour before they have to surface and breathe.

Capybara

The prize for the principal grazer of the floating meadows goes to the capybara *Hydrochaeris hydrochaeris*, a remarkable animal that also takes the title of world's largest rodent. Rodents, the most diverse order of mammals on the planet, are defined by their teeth, specifically the large pair of chisel-like incisors in the front of each jaw, which have evolved into a bewildering variety of weapons depending on the food niche being exploited. In the capybara, these have been allied to a bulging

The jaguar (*Panthera onca*) is a good swimmer; at Mamirauá, it feeds mainly on the spectacled caiman that it stalks on the shores of lakes and channels. With luck, both the spotted and the dark forms (bottom, photo taken at CIGS Zoo, Manaus) can be seen at Mamirauá.

set of jaw muscles and a number of adaptations to a semi-aquatic lifestyle to earn the title 'master of the grasses', the meaning of the indigenous word *capybara.*

Capybara seem more comfortable in the water than out of it, and much of their lives take place in the rivers and lakes of the *várzea*. They are able to feed on aquatic plants standing on the bottom, they will bask in the shallows to escape the midday heat, and they will take immediately to water at any sign of danger. Even mating takes place in the water, with the female often being entirely submerged in a particularly vigorous episode. They are most often seen either in the shallows at the side of watercourses, or crossing rivers, when you may get a glimpse of rodent-like eyes and ears, all set high on the head to allow a good view whilst waterborne, before they dive out of sight. Partially webbed feet mean the capybara is an excellent swimmer: expect them to resurface some distance away.

Capybara are cavimorph rodents, from the original rodent fauna of South America, and thus related to the agoutis and the pacas, primarily *terra firme* animals, as well as to the guinea pigs of the Andes. Like them, capybara are prized as game animals, though the meat is strongly flavoured with more than a tang of the *capim* or floating grass on which they graze so heavily. Hunting has made capybara scarce and shy along many of the waterways that are their main home. In some parts of South America, capybara are managed sustainably for their meat and hides: their high reproduction rates and large size, up to 50kg, make this a viable proposition.

Jaguar

Capybara are a prey species of the *várzea's* top predator, the fabled *onça* or jaguar *Panthera onca*. Only the very patient or very lucky can hope for a glimpse of this elusive cat. 'Jaguar are only seen after many hundreds of hours of observation in the field,' comments Márcio Ayres, whose sightings have included the rare black form. Mamirauá certainly supports a population of these magnificent animals, and it is not uncommon to come across the characteristic pugmark, on beaches or in the soft leaf litter of *restinga* trails. Like many other cats, jaguar like to use man made trails at night. They are at home in the *várzea*, frequenting wet and waterside habitat where they hunt capybara, caiman and the *jaboti* tortoise. If the need arises, they are excellent swimmers, and fish make up a large part of the diet. Fabled for their cunning, a *ribeirinho* story has the jaguar using the tip of his tail to simulate falling fruit and lure the fish within reach of his claws. Another graceful predator of the *várzea* lakes and streams is the river otter *Lutra longicaudis*. Awkward and hump-backed on land, in the water otters are fast and efficient predators of fish and crustaceans.

Many years ago the giant Brazilian otter (*Pteronura brasilensis*) became extinct at Mamirauá, but the elegant river otter (*Lutra longicaudis*) can still be seen in the channels and more remote lakes.

The vampire bat (*Desmodus rotundus*), above, feeds on blood, mainly from domestic animals.

The long-nosed bat (*Rhynchonycteris naso*) is often seen resting on the shingles of the verandas at Uakari Floating Lodge.

Bats

Second only to rodents in diversity, bats in the order Chiroptera are another group of mammals that are at their most diverse and extraordinary in the neotropical rainforests, though little is as yet known about their particular adaptations to life in the *várzea*.

New World bats are a fine example of adaptive radiation, branching out from insectivorous ancestors to fill a host of other ecological niches. Many species of bats exploit the plentiful resources of fruit, nectar and pollen provided by the rainforest, and adaptations in several *várzea* plants, such as flower clusters near natural landing pads at the end of branches, or stout stalks, suggest a co-evolutionary, mutually beneficial relationship. The grandest of the *várzea* trees, the samaumeira *Ceiba pentandra*, is bat-pollinated.

Others bats have adopted more predatory practices. The largest neotropical bat is *Vampyrum spectrum*, whose fearsome appearance and 70cm wingspan prompted Bates to comment 'nothing in animal physiognomy can be more hideous than the countenance of this creature', and led many early observers to conclude that this must be the bloodsucker of legend. In fact, the false vampire, as it is now known, is a proficient hunter of birds, rodents and other bats. Like all neotropical bats, *Vampyrum* uses echo-location to navigate and find prey in the tropical night, and its outsize ears make excellent receptors for returning signals. An even more accomplished echo-locater is the greater fishing bulldog bat *Noctilio leporinus*, whose sonar equipment can detect the ripples caused by fish just below the surface whilst flying over lakes or rivers. The bat then swoops down and gaffs its prey with sharply clawed feet.

Perhaps the most infamous of neotropical bats is diminutive by comparison, finds its meal largely by smell, and approaches its prey on all fours. Once in position on the sleeping capybara, cow or occasional unfortunate human, *Desmodus rotundus* makes a small and painless incision in the skin with razor sharp teeth. Injecting anti-coagulant saliva to keep the blood flowing, the little bat laps its fill. Naturally rare, *Desmodus* is becoming more common where *várzea* cattle ranching provides large concentrations of food. Despite its slightly unsavoury habits, *Desmodus* is a model of social responsibility where its fellow bloodsuckers are concerned. Engorged vampires will regurgitate blood to roost mates who fail to find food in a behaviour known to biologists as reciprocal altruism, a rational strategy when meals are copious but hard to find, and more than 72 hours without sustenance spells doom for the little bat.

THE BANQUET OF THE WATERS

For the fruit eating arboreal mammals and herbivorous manatees, high water in Mamirauá brings abundant food supplies, when reserves are built up against the lean times when the floods subside. The seasons have a very different meaning for the inhabitants of the reserve, including man, who depend on fish for most or all of their diet. During the floods their prey disperses into the forest and is hard to find and catch. But when the waters fall the fish become concentrated in the lakes, to be joined by the recently hatched young of the numerous species who reproduce at this time of year. The result is an astonishing demonstration of the productivity of the *várzea* ecosystem. The water seems to boil with fish, and residents of nearby communities talk of scooping them up in handfuls. For the fish predators, this is a time of plenty, and they arrive in force.

Caiman

An hour after sunset, and the sky is quite dark, with the Southern Cross clear on the horizon and the moon, yet to rise, casting a glow on the eastern sky. As your guide cuts the motor and allows the canoe to drift gently towards the bank, you can hear the final mutterings of some of the diurnal fauna, the chirruping of a group of squirrel monkeys in their sleeping tree. Otherwise, silence; the bank seems uninhabited. Then he switches on his torch.

Ronis da Silveira, a specialist in caimans at INPA in Manaus and a researcher at Mamirauá since 1993, describes a flashlight cruise of Lago Mamirauá during the dry season as 'like Rio de Janeiro by night'. All the way along the bank, red eyes by the thousand reflect the torch beam, motionless until you get too close and they vanish as their owner slips silently beneath the surface.

As the dry season approaches, flocks of herons, cormorants and other aquatic birds gather to eat fish that are trapped in the shallow, temporary ponds.

In the dry season, thousands of black caimans gather in Mamirauá Lake. At night, the eyes of these animals reflect the flashlight beams and the lake "looks like Rio de Janeiro seen from Guanabara Bay".
The black caiman (above and center) likes to stay in the water, while the spectacled caiman prefers the shores of the lake.

Crocodilians are the last terrestrial remnants of the giant reptiles of the Mesozoic era that included the dinosaurs, and fossil records show that they have changed little in the last 80 million years.

With four species, the Amazon basin is one of the major centres of crocodilian diversity in the world, and three of these species are present in Mamirauá, though the naturally rare and secretive Cuvier's dwarf caiman *Paleosuchus palpebrosus* is unlikely to be seen on a short visit. Alligators and caiman are distinguished from true crocodiles by the fourth tooth on the lower jaw, which is not visible when the animal closes its mouth, though with seventy-two teeth in all close range counting is probably better left to the experts.

The two species of caiman the visitor is likely to see at Mamirauá are relatively easily distinguished. Over 2.5m in length and you are looking at the black caiman *Melanosuchus niger*, with its more massive black head, black back and black and white banded tail. Male black caiman can attain 6m and weigh more than 200kg, making them the most massive predator in continental America. The spectacled caiman *Caiman crocodilus crocodilus* is much smaller and lighter, and its skin is a yellowish 'beer' colour. Any caiman seen on land is likely to be *C. crocodilus*; in the same way a caiman seen in open water in one of the *várzea* lakes is much more likely to be *M. niger*.

Caiman are opportunist and generalist predators. Young caiman subsist mainly on insects, but adults will take almost all of the invertebrate and vertebrate fauna of Mamirauá, including crabs, snakes, spiders, snails and even, on occasion, other caiman. Cannibalism is thought to act as a natural control on the caiman population, and is more common in the dry season when they become hugely concentrated in the *várzea* lakes. A resident of the Reserve told Da Silveira he had seen a black caiman swimming with a dead young uakari in its jaws. But for the caiman of Mamirauá, the most important food resource is fish, and particularly the massive stocks of fish confined to the *várzea* lakes during the period of low water. Crocodilians have an extraordinary metabolism with very low energetic demands, and after gorging themselves on this dry season banquet, the caiman of Mamirauá eat relatively little for the rest of the year.

During high water the caiman disperse into the flooded forest, but the females remain close to their breeding lakes, and in August when the waters begin to fall, they begin the construction of their nests. A circular structure roughly 1.5m in diameter made of leaves and plant material, black caiman nests can be seen close to *restinga* trails in the Ecotourism zone, though never very far from water. Care must be taken whilst the female is on the nest, however, as she will vigorously defend the

Some females, like this one who attacked the photographer during a photo session, defend their nest, but this is very rare behavior at Mamirauá.

At right, a newborn black caiman ecloding from the egg and, below, a baby black caiman in the water near the nest.

clutch of up to 45 eggs against nest predators that include lizards, jaguar, capuchin monkeys and people. Incubation takes roughly 90 days, during which one of the most peculiar aspects of caiman biology is played out. Like some other reptiles, crocodilians have no sex chromosomes: that is, no genetic codes for the gender of their young. Instead, the temperature during incubation is the determining factor. In this way, the construction of the nest and the level of sunlight it receives influence the number of male and female young that will hatch. The female often has to break the walls of the nest to permit her brood to escape, and will sometimes carry the tiny caiman in her jaws to the nearby water.

Early counts of caiman in Amazonia were carried out along the banks of the great rivers, where the black caiman is naturally scarce, and led to concern that the species was under threat of extinction. Today it is known that the black caiman prefers the more enclosed habitats of the *várzea*, such as at Mamirauá, with calm lakes free from the strong currents of the main channels. Researchers at Mamirauá believe that exploitation of caiman products may prove sustainable if properly managed, and are examining how the people of Mamirauá could profit legally from the responsible use of these remarkable reptiles.

Dolphin

A 'huff' of exhaled air on the other side of the canoe, and you turn just in time to see a pair of dorsal fins vanish below the surface, a sign that the caiman have competition at the banquet. Dolphins have successfully colonized many of the world's large river systems, and Mamirauá has two species that make the most of the abundance of fish at low water.

The boto or pink river dolphin *Inia geoffrensis*, endemic to the Amazon and Orinoco river basins, is a member of the Platanistoidae. This 'super family' also includes the river dolphins of the Yangtze in China and the Ganges, Indus and other rivers in India, Pakistan, Bangladesh and Nepal. *Inia* is likely to be the senior of the two Amazon dolphins, with some evidence to suggest that the ancestors of today's botos entered from the Pacific before the rising Andes sealed off the basin. The tucuxi *Sotalia fluviatilis*, by contrast, is still partly a marine animal, with two distinct forms being recognised within the species. One is limited to the freshwater system, whilst the other is found in the estuarine and coastal waters around the mouth of the Amazon and elsewhere on the Atlantic coast of South America.

When you see your first boto it is often hard to believe that any animal, particularly such a voracious predator, could be bright lipstick pink. Male botos can be particularly vivid, though the normally grey tucuxi can also display a ventral blush at times. The colour is caused by blood flow in tiny capillaries beneath the skin, and seems to be related to sexual maturity and activity. There appears to be a relationship with water turbidity also: dolphins that live in muddy rivers tend to be pinker, whilst animals kept in clear water in captivity lose their colouration over time.

Another clue to the history of the two Amazon dolphins is found in the bones of their necks. In the tucuxi, as in most modern dolphins, the vertebrae have become fused, reducing the flexibility of the head and neck but increasing its rigidity and resistance in the leaps and acrobatics that dolphins are so famous for. The boto, in contrast, retains a degree of movement. It is much less inclined to leap out of the water, in consequence, but uses its extra flexibility to manoeuvre through the maze of submerged vegetation to find food in the flooded forest at high water. Tucuxis, for their part, seem to avoid any shallow or enclosed waterway, and never enter the flooded forest itself. Botos are heavy and corpulent, males reaching 200 kg in weight, and their dorsal fin is low and elongated, more like a keel than the shark-like fin of the marine dolphins. Tucuxi are much smaller, about 50kg for an adult, and can easily be identified by their characteristic triangular and hooked dorsal fin.

The behaviour of the Mamirauá river dolphins has been under study since 1994: no easy task, as individuals and even genders are very hard to distinguish in the muddy waters of the *várzea* lakes. Using special marking techniques and in some cases the fitting of radio transmitters, the research program is beginning to shed some light on the life history of the boto and tucuxi. Botos in particular seem to be great generalists, feeding in rivers, lakes, forest and floating meadows depending on the location of their prey, and moving seasonally to follow migrating fish. Though these voyages may cover hundreds of kilometres, the study shows that Mamirauá dolphins generally return, and that the reserve seems to have a particular importance as an area for reproduction and as a refuge for mothers with calves.

Gestation in the boto is about 10-11 months, and most births occur between June and September as the water level falls in Mamirauá. Calves normally remain with their mothers for 2-3 years, and become increasingly independent as they grow. The boto study is now following the progress of more than 60 individually-marked adult females, and visitors may well see some of these animals with their youngsters in close attendance. Individuals "F", "Y" and "S" have produced more than one calf during the period of the study, and each new sighting brings with it the exciting possibility of the appearance of a new baby. Visitors can contribute to this important work by noting the mark on dolphins seen, together with the location of the sighting, and recording the observation in the book provided at the Lodge.

Male botos and tucuxis have very different strategies for ensuring that their

The pink dolphin (*Inia geoffrensis*) coming to the surface to breathe (above).
Visitors can observe the dorsal fin at water level (right).

The animal is captured for marking, and then returned to the water.

genes pass into the next generation of river dolphins. When female botos come into oestrus, the males in an area will fight for the right to mate with them, and individuals often show the scars of battle. Tucuxi, on the other hand, operate a seemingly peaceful system of polyandry, where females mate with several different males. The relative size of tucuxi testes, however, indicates that the genetic struggle is being fought out at the microscopic level, in what biologists call 'sperm competition'. Gestation in the tucuxi is similar to that of the boto, but birth is timed to occur at low water.

Aquatic birds

Early morning, and the sound of beating wings announces the arrival of another of the dry season visitors to the lakes of Mamirauá. The first to abandon their night-time roosts are wary and circle the lake before alighting, but soon wave after wave are splashing down until the lake is black with flapping, ducking and squawking birds. Whilst Mamirauá is year round home to many resident aquatic species, the advent of the dry season and the concentration of food provided by the *várzea* lakes at low water coincides with arrival of many seasonal migrants from other parts of Amazonia and further afield.

Most conspicuous in sheer numbers is the neotropic cormorant *Phalacrocorax brasilianus*. Seen in their thousands floating on the *várzea* lakes, perched in waterside trees or occasionally flying in arrowhead formation over the canopy, they are locally known as *mergulhão* or diver, in testament to their underwater abilities. Cormorants pursue and catch their prey underwater, using webbed feet to propel themselves and the tail as an improvised rudder. A downward hook at the tip of the beak prevents breakfast from escaping once seized, and cormorants are commonly seen at the surface painstakingly manoeuvring their prey into the right orientation for swallowing. Sometimes mistaken for a cormorant but slightly larger with a longer neck and fan-shaped tail, the darter *Anhinga anhinga* shares the characteristic wing-drying posture, and also dives for fish, though the very thin and pointed bill is used to impale prey before bringing it to the surface.

The shallower waters at the lake's edge are patrolled for fish, frogs and other prey by the herons, egrets and bitterns of the Ardeidae family. Largest amongst them is the white-necked heron *Ardea cocoi*, a large blue-grey heron often seen flying away from the edge of Mamirauá watercourses with slow and deliberate wing beats at the approach of a boat. *Ardea* nests in noisy colonies at various points in the reserve, and is sometimes kept by local people in their homes, both as an unlikely pet and eventually for the pot. More numerous are the egrets

In the dry season, thousands of Brazilian cormorants (*Phalacrocorax brasilianus*) come to feast on the fish of Mamirauá Lake.

An anhinga (*Anhinga anhinga*), drying its wings.

The elegant sunbittern is often spotted on the shores of Mamirauá Lake.

The white-necked heron, the largest of all herons, is a solitary bird.

The adult and immature stages of the rufescent tiger heron are not recognized by the local people at Mamirauá.
They think they are different species.

Egrets also come for the banquet of the waters. They come by the thousands to Mamirauá Lake.

Egretta spp., who often provide a thrilling escort as they fly alongside the boat, their white plumage in dramatic contrast to the forest behind. Also white but with a distinctive blue face and two handsome white head plumes is the capped heron *Pilherodius pileatus*.

There are several other species of heron, but they are more cryptic in colouration and secretive in habits. The grey-green striated heron *Butorides striatus* crouches motionless for long periods before a lightening jab secures its prey. The rufescent tiger heron *Tigrisoma lineatum* is named after the fine barring or tiger-stripes of its plumage. Strangest of all is the boat-billed heron *Cochlearius cochlearius* seldom seen because of its nocturnal habits but unmistakable given its wide and flattened, boat-like bill. Speculation over the purpose of this equipment includes courtship display or specialised feeding, but a lack of evidence means it remains a mystery.

The elegant sunbittern *Eurypyga helias* stalks insects, little fish and amphibians, and its low, whistled call is heard at dawn and dusk near water. A display of the inside of its wings shows a flash of bright colours, but the plumage otherwise is patterned and cryptic.

Both the ringed-kingfisher *Ceryle torquata* (left) and the Amazon kingfisher *Chloroceryle amazona* (swallowing a fish) perch on branches overlooking the water, from where they dive and capture their prey.

The black skimmer (*Rynchops niger*) swoops low over the lake with its mandible, which is larger than the maxilla, slicing through the water to capture prey (small fish and shrimp).

Large-billed terns (*Phaetusa simplex*) enjoy perching on floating logs or those mired in the shallows.

Of the five species of kingfishers or Alcinidae present in Mamirauá, by far the most often seen is the ringed kingfisher *Ceryle torquata*, identified by its large size and blueish grey colouration with a rufous breast and white neck. This kingfisher is noisy and conspicuous, often in swooping flight over water making its characteristic 'chick-chick' call. Like all kingfishers it dives for fish from favoured perches on branches overhanging the water, and possesses a specially adapted retina to offset the effects of refraction when zeroing-in on prey beneath the surface. The other four species are iridescent green with rufous breasts, and vary in size down to the tiny pygmy kingfisher *Chloroceryle aenea*, a mere 13cm, which feeds on small fish, tadpoles and insects. Another accomplished diver is the large-billed tern *Phaetusa simplex*, known as *gaivota* in Amazonia, though this word can mean seagull in other parts of Brazil. Terns dive for fish from a hovering position a few metres above the surface, and also prey on hatchling river turtles as they race from nest to water.

NON-AQUATIC BIRDS

The flooded forest provides unique opportunities for aquatic birds, but the *várzea* avifauna also exploits the abundance of fruit, insects and other food sources. However, researchers believe that the diversity of bird species at Mamirauá is lower than in surrounding area of *terra firme* forest, albeit higher than in other areas of *várzea* further down the river's course. In fact, many species use both systems, sometimes on a daily basis: flight diminishes the obstacles presented by wide rivers and other natural barriers. Weak fliers, or birds whose ecological niche is the forest floor, subject to annual inundation in the reserve, are either absent from Mamirauá or have found interesting solutions to the challenge of *várzea* life.

The undulated tinamou *Crypturellus undulatus*, like the other species of the genus, forages in the leaf litter and undergrowth, and relies on cryptic colouring to protect it from predators. Tinamous are shy and very difficult to see, especially as they prefer to remain motionless or sneak away when danger threatens. Only if approached very closely will they flush on whirring wings, though they can only manage a flight of thirty metres or so. Their presence in seasonally flooded *várzea* is thus something of a puzzle. The solution may lie in observations of *Crypturellus* swimming across the major rivers bordering the reserve. Faced with the loss of their habitat as the waters rise, and lacking the ability to reach dry land on the wing, it appears the tinamous make this hazardous crossing, at least in years of high floods, to wait out the flood in the *terra firme* forest before returning to re-colonize the *várzea* when the waters subside.

Another weak flier is the curassow, although this gallinaceous bird can usually manage to flap across the channels between *restingas*, its favoured habitat. Two species occur in Mamirauá: the razor-billed curassow *Mitu tuberosa*, present throughout the basin; and the rare and little known wattled curassow *Crax globulosa*.

The scarlet macaw *Ara macao* is, without a doubt, one of the most beautiful birds in the world.

An undulated tinamou (*Crypturellus undulatus*) crossing the Japurá River to escape from the rising floodwaters of the Mamirauá varzea.

Razor-billed curassow (*Mitu tuberosa*), center, left.

Visitors will certainly hear the voice of the horned screamer (*Anhima cornuta*) reverberating across the lakes of the Reserve.

The bare-necked fruit crow (*Gymnoderus foetidus*), flying high over forest and water, is a common sight.

Outside the *várzea* curassow will forage for fallen fruit on the ground, but in the flooded forest they seem to have adopted a more strictly arboreal lifestyle. Turkey like in size and taste, the high regard in which the curassow is held as a game bird has led to heavy hunting pressure, especially close to settlements. Mamirauá may now support one of the most important populations of these birds in the region.

Untroubled by the hunters is the peculiar horned screamer *Anhima cornuta*, whose flesh has a disagreeable spongy texture owing to the presence of air spaces between skin and muscle, perhaps an aerodynamic adaptation, as these bulky birds are accomplished fliers and can soar to great heights. Their name refers both to the distinctive quill projecting from the head and the piercing call that rolls over the *várzea* lakes at dusk. *Anhima* seems to favour the swampy *chavascal*, and feeds on aquatic grasses and plants such as the water hyacinth.

Parrots and Macaws

Fruit is abundant in the várzea, but it still takes a bit of finding. Rainforest fruit is what biologists call a 'patchy' resource: only certain kinds of fruit are available in a given location at a given season, and the frugivore must find the right tree at the right time in order to secure a meal. For this reason, a fruit diet tends to select for social behaviour. A large flock can locate fruiting trees more easily, and once the feast is found, there is generally enough for everyone.

The parrots and their relatives in the family Psittacidae are amongst the most gregarious of birds, and with nineteen species, Mamirauá has the highest diversity of any conservation area in the world. Most parrots are green and can be surprisingly hard to see in the canopy, but they are never hard to hear. The noise of a flock of a typical várzea species, the festive parrot *Amazona festiva,* feeding in one of their favourite trees such as the piranheira, can be ear-splitting: a chorus of raucous squawks as the birds clamber about in the branches, using their powerful beaks as a third limb in their acrobatic manoeuvres as well as to split the fruit and crush the seeds. The piranheira tree gains nothing from its noisy visitors: parrots are major seed predators on more than a dozen várzea trees.

Parrots can live remarkably long lives, and most species are monogamous, forming pair bonds which are reinforced by mutual preening and which may last for life. The magnificent macaws, of which Mamirauá has three species, are invariably seen in pairs, crossing the rivers and lakes at dawn and dusk in stately flight, so close that their wingtips seem to touch. Macaws favour riverside trees as their roosting sites, but 'commute' to other areas of the várzea, or sometimes to the *terra firme,* to feed during the day. They are the largest of the parrots: the scarlet macaw

Festive parrots abound at Mamirauá; the river people like to keep them as pets. Mamirauá is world champion in parrot diversity, with 19 recorded species.

The blue-and-yellow macaw *Ara ararauna* and the red-and-green macaw *Ara chloroptera*, are magnificent examples of the beauty of Neotropical wildlife.

Ara macao can measure 85 cm and weigh more than a kilogram. Their magnificent plumage is created by a combination of pigments in the feathers, which provide the reds and yellows, and the fine structure of the barbs themselves, which reflect light in such a way as to give the blues and greens and metallic sheens. A flight of macaws overhead at sunset, calling to each other with a harsh 'rraa…aah', is one of the finest sights of the *várzea*.

Toucans

A diet of fruit alone provides plenty of carbohydrate but is low in protein, and for this reason many fruit eaters supplement their diet with insect or animal food. The toucans, from the family Ramphastidae, will occasionally eat lizards and small animals, and have even been observed to attack nests and take eggs and young birds, though fruit remains the main component of their diet. One of the best known of rainforest birds, toucans are unmistakable, whether seen in swooping, undulating flight over rivers and lakes, or in the branches of favourite trees such as the figs *Ficus* spp.

The purpose of their giant bills, which can seem to be as large as the bird and are often brightly coloured, remains unclear. Bates believed it was an adaptation to allow the toucan to reach fruit on outlying branches that would not support the weight of the heavy bird. Other writers have suggested the bill is a defensive weapon, and that the bright colouration acts as a warning to predators. The bill itself is surprisingly light, made up of a honeycomb structure of bony struts and fibrous tissue similar to a fingernail. Toucans show great skill in manipulating their food with such an unwieldy piece of cutlery, picking selected fruit with the tip and then tossing it backwards and gulping it down. Unlike parrots, however, they seem reluctant to swallow seeds, and will often spit them up, thus playing an important role in the seed dispersal of many *várzea* trees.

Mamirauá provides a protected habitat for three species of toucan *Ramphastos* spp., and three more of the closely related aracari *Pteroglossus* spp. The situation was very different in nineteenth century Tefé, then called Ega, when during the high water season Bates reports that 'everyone…who can get a gun of any sort and a few charges of powder and shot, or a blow-pipe, goes daily to the woods to kill a few brace for dinner; for … the people of Ega live almost exclusively on stewed and roasted Toucans during the months of June and July; the birds being then very fat, and the meat exceedingly sweet and tender.'

At left: The red-billed toucan *Ramphastos tucanus*.

Manakins

Once the right trees have been found, fruit requires comparatively little effort from the frugivore: it does not run away, nor is it cunningly camouflaged. You might think of the fruit eaters therefore as the playboys of the rainforest avifauna, and they do seem to have more 'free time' than specialists of other ecological niches, much of which is invested in activities connected with breeding. Good examples are the manakins of the family Pipridae, a group of small, chubby birds represented by three species in Mamirauá, whose fruit diet is supplemented by insects.

Many manakin species exhibit extraordinary mating behaviour characterised by communal 'dancing' by the brightly coloured males, in seeming competition for assisting females. Male manakins may spend most of their adult lives at these performances, or 'leks', whilst the females, having chosen a mate according the complex rules of dominance established by the dancing birds, take on all the responsibility of nesting and raising young. The male of one of the Mamirauá species, the wire-tailed manakin *Pipra filicauda,* complements the effect of his dance by brushing females under the chin with his fine tail filaments. Stranger still, many manakin males continue to dance when no females are present, in a sort of dress rehearsal for future performances. Lekking behaviour is exhibited by other tropical birds, and indeed by birds and mammals all over the world, and its evolutionary origins are still the subject of debate amongst biologists.

Caciques and Oropendolas

The most distinctive nests in Mamirauá belong to the caciques *Cacicus* spp. and the oropendolas *Psarocolius* spp., of the family Icteridae and relatives of the blackbird. Hanging from a tall tree over looking the river channel or lakeshore are twenty or more pendulous, woven baskets, usually the centre of much activity as the colony goes about its construction work or prepares for a feeding foray on the fruit and nectar of the nearby forest.

Living in these close packed communities confers a certain amount of protection from predators, and each bird tries to construct its nest in the centre of the colony where the threat of attack is lowest. The oropendola's main protection, however, comes from the neighbours: colonies are almost invariably sited close to nests of stinging ants or wasps, whose attentions discourage would-be predators from approaching too closely.

At right: the elusive sungrebe *Heliornis fulica.*

A male yellow-rumped cacique displays on its nest as a female looks on and another female weaves her own nest.

Above:
Left: red-capped cardinal (*Paroaria gularis*).
Right: The only South American animal that has truly been domesticated is the muscovy duck (*Cairina moschata*).

Tyrant Flycatchers

With its astonishing diversity of insect life, it is no surprise that the rainforest supports a wide variety of bird species adapted to feed on them. Perhaps the most successful, and certainly the most numerous, are the tyrant flycatchers, whose family Tyrannidae includes a baffling 393 identified species. One of the most familiar is the kiskadee *Pitangus sulphuratus*, whose striped head and lemon yellow breast are known from South Texas to Argentina, as much from towns and gardens as from the rainforest. Its Brazilian name is derived from its insistent call, whose syllables mimic the phrase '*bem-te-vi'*, or 'nice to see you'. The tyrant flycatchers are an impressive example of what biologists call adaptive radiation. From the basic model, which as its name suggests caught insects on the wing, new species have evolved to pursue a myriad of alternative strategies, including abandoning insects altogether and eating fruit instead. In Mamirauá alone, 49 species have been recorded.

Woodpeckers and Woodcreepers

The woodpeckers or Picidae, a familiar and worldwide family represented in Mamirauá by eleven species, occupy another insectivorous niche. Woodpeckers climb vertically up the trunk of *várzea* trees using stiffened tail feathers as a prop, and probe or bore the bark for insects and grubs. When prey is located it is extracted from its hiding place using the woodpecker's extremely long forked tongue. Perhaps the most showy of the *várzea* species is the cream-coloured woodpecker *Celeus flavus*, which is a brilliant yellow buff in colour with a crimson moustache.

If one family can evolve to exploit many different ecological niches, like the tyrant flycatchers, then quite distinct families can adapt to the needs of similar habitats. This is known as evolutionary convergence, and the woodcreepers of the family Dendrocolaptidae are good examples. Like woodpeckers, they have the long beak and stiffened tail feathers required for a life of trunk poking, but are no relation to that family, being instead descended from the ovenbirds, a family of quite different habits.

The most commonly seen is the plain-brown woodcreeper *Dendrocincla fuliginosa*, which forages methodically from the base to the tops of trees. *Dendrocincla* will often abandon its arboreal habits, however, to join the mixed assemblage of birds that act as camp followers to the army ants *Eciton* spp., feeding not on the ants themselves but on the invertebrates flushed from their hiding places by advancing columns. Bates made a detailed study of these ants, and when searching for them on the forest floor found 'the first signal given… is the twittering and restless movement of small flocks of plain coloured birds.'

The crimson-crested woodpecker (*Campephilus melanoleucus*) dining on cecropia ants.

Center: the lesser kiskadee (*Philohydor lictor*) is fairly common on the shores of Mamirauá (left).
The orange-fronted yellow-finch (*Sicalis columbiana*), at right, is usualy seen on the floating meadows.

Birds of the floating meadows in song: the yellow-hooded blackbird (*Agelaius icterocephalus*), at left, and the black-capped donacobius (*Donacobius atricapillus*).

Vultures and birds of prey

Almost certainly the first of the many and varied birds of prey of Amazonia that the visitor will encounter is the black vulture *Coragyps atratus*. Every morning in towns across the region thousands of bags of garbage are put out on the street to await an often erratic municipal disposal system, and every morning thousands of black vultures swoop down to begin the job themselves. Vultures have specialized digestive systems that enable them to neutralize the harmful bacteria found in decaying animal matter. These large and rather ugly birds are a familiar site in Tefé, thrusting their naked heads into the rubbish in search of scraps or thronging the roofs of the town, drying their wings in the sun after a cloudburst. In Mamirauá, four other species of vulture patrol the *várzea* for carrion, including the spectacular king vulture *Sarcoramphus papa*, black and white with prominent orange wattles.

Along the banks of the rivers and lakes, the screeching call of the black-collared hawk *Busarellus nigricollis* is a familiar and haunting sound. Chestnut coloured with a creamy white head and a distinctive black patch on the breast, this hawk is almost always seen perched over the water, from where it swoops to catch fish and frogs. Local people call it the *gavião panema*, *panema* being the mysterious influence certain animals and people are thought to wield over the success of a day's fishing. The most powerful bird of prey of the *várzea*, and indeed of the world, is sometimes seen in Mamirauá. The harpy eagle *Harpia harpyja* stands a metre high with an unmistakable blackish crest, and hunts monkeys and sloths in the canopy.

Two oddities

Mamirauá also offers the opportunity to see two of the most peculiar of the world's birds. About the size of a crow, the Amazonian umbrella bird *Cephalopterus ornatus* is a member of the cotinga family, and feeds on large insects and fruits. It is rare, but favours the margins of rivers and lakes and is sometimes seen crossing the watercourses in Mamirauá. Its name comes from the crest of black feathers that adorns its head like a pudding bowl haircut. Displaying males make a distinctive 'boom' rather like the lowing of a bull, which carries for long distances.

The extraordinary hoatzin *Opisthocomus hoazin* (pages10/11) also sports a crest, and like the umbrella bird it favours the *Cecropia* groves in the lower lying areas of the flooded forest. Hoatzins are among the few birds that eat leaves, and they have an enlarged crop where their often toxic food is allowed to partially decompose before digestion, giving the hoatzin colony its distinctive, cow manure odour. They are comically poor fliers, but hoatzin chicks are strong swimmers, and when threatened employ the unique strategy of toppling from the nest into the water beneath, from where they swim to the nearest tree and clamber out using claws at the bend of each wing.

The great potoo (*Nyctibius grandis*), is not rare, but it is a master of camouflage.

The black-collared hawk (*Busarellus nigricollis*), at right, is fairly common on the shores of the lakes.

Harpy eagles (*Harpia harpyja*) have been seen many times at Mamirauá.

REPTILES AND AMPHIBIANS

Turtles

If the season of low water is a time of plenty for one group of large reptiles, the caiman, it is no less important in the life history of another of the ancient users of the reserve, the river turtles. The large freshwater turtles of Amazonia, unlike most living turtles, do not retract their heads backwards but tuck them to the side when danger threatens. Side-necks, as they are called, are thought to date from the Mesozoic era, and until historic times were extremely numerous throughout the Upper Amazon. Although numbers were already in decline by Bates' time, a result of the heavy trade in oil rendered from turtle eggs, he reports that at low water the beaches around Tefé would be black with turtles. 'The Indians,' he reports, 'say that formerly the waters teemed as thickly with turtles as the air now does with mosquitoes.'

Bates was talking about the tartaruga, the giant Amazon river turtle *Podocnemis expansa*. The tartaruga is the largest freshwater turtle present at Mamirauá, with the larger females attaining 75kg and a metre in length. Once an important component of the diet of the *ribeirinho* and a valuable economic resource, stocks have declined so drastically that the smaller turtles are now more significant. An illegal trade in tartaruga continues, however, generally for its meat, which commands high prices and is sought after for special occasions.

Next in size come the tracajá *Podocnemis unifilis* and the matamatá *Chelus fimbriatus*, a turtle with a long snake-like neck and strange pointed keels on its carapace that serve as camouflage as it lies in ambush on the bottom of the *várzea* water bodies. But the most abundant of the Mamirauá turtles is the little iaçá

The voice of the frog (*Hyla leucophyllata*) is one of the first sounds heard at Mamirauá as night falls. The iguana (*Iguana iguana*) is often seen basking in the sun on the shores of Mamirauá Lake.

The iaçá turtle has been the subject of much research at Mamirauá since 1996.

The tracajá, with characteristic yellow marks on its head, and the giant Amazon river turtle (above), are other fresh water species.

The yellow-footed tortoise (*Geochelone denticulata*) is basically a land animal, but surprisingly, it is also quite common at Mamirauá.

Podocnemis sextuberculata, which has been the subject of a research program within the reserve since 1996.

To understand iaçá ecology, the turtles are captured with nets, weighed, measured and tagged before being released. From then on, the project relies on the assistance of local people, who are asked to hand over for analysis any tagged turtles they find or catch. Researchers can then piece together the information and begin to shed some light on the seasonal movements of the turtles, their feeding habits and reproductive behaviour.

During the high water seasons the turtles disperse throughout the flooded forest, feeding on seeds and fruits, and to a lesser extent on fish, insects and crustaceans. In September, the female iaçá arrive at sandy beaches recently exposed by the retreating water. The first of the turtle species to arrive, the iaçá minimize the chance that their nests will be flooded again before the eggs have hatched. The females ascend the beach at night and dig holes in the sand with their rear flippers. Between 6 and 25 eggs are deposited before the nests are covered over again. Even so, predators such as the tegu lizard *Tupinambis teguixin* find and destroy many eggs, and the nests are attacked by the larvae of the Sarcophagidae fly. Those that survive hatch in November, and the young turtles run the gauntlet of terns and other predators to reach the water. Even there they are not safe, as the commotion attracts the attention of piranha. Many mature turtles show the scars of piranha attack in mutilations to the flippers. Nonetheless, man remains the greatest turtle predator and the main threat to the continued existence of these species throughout the Amazon. In Mamirauá, the 4th General Assembly prohibited the use of gill nets to catch turtles off nesting beaches during the breeding season, and several communities have set aside beaches as protected areas for turtle reproduction.

Not everything in a shell in Mamirauá is a turtle. The yellow-footed tortoise *Geochelone denticulata* is primarily an animal of the *terra firme* forest but seems to have adapted to life in the *várzea* and takes advantage of its food resources. These *jabuti*, as they are locally known, often get trapped on the higher *restingas* by the rising floodwater, and are an important food source for jaguar and also for man.

Lizards

Tupinambis is one of three large lizards of the family Teiidae to make their home in the *várzea*. The other two are further adapted to an aquatic lifestyle, showing the flattened tail and ridged scales that caiman also employ to improve their swimming ability, which similarity may give rise to their names, the caiman lizard *Dracaena guianensis* and the jacarerana or false caiman *Crocodilurus lacertinus*. Both can reach a metre in length. Known locally, and confusingly, as a chameleon, but quite distinct from those African animals, is the familiar iguana *Iguana iguana*. Also excellent swimmers, iguana nonetheless live primarily an arboreal existence, and can be seen basking in the upper branches of waterside trees. When danger threatens, however, they take to the water, making dramatic dives of ten metres or more, and breaking the fall with their strong tails. They are also distinguished by their vegetarian diet of fruit and leaves, but though a potentially useful protein source and a dietary component across much of Latin America, they are not widely relished in Mamirauá. Two smaller *várzea* lizards, *Kentropyx altamazonica* and *Uranoscodon superciliosus*, have the surprising ability to run for brief periods across the surface of the water, a trick generally employed to escape predators.

Snakes

As for Amazonia as a whole, the majority of Mamirauá's snake population is made up of innocuous and rather beautiful snakes from the family Colubridae, most of which are non-venomous. The vine snakes are members of this family; whip-thin snakes that patrol the canopy for small birds and lizards. *Oxybelis fulgidus* is a particularly handsome example, vivid green in colour, whilst *Chironius fuscus* is more grey-brown and feeds primarily on amphibians.

Other Colubrid snakes have evolved a completely aquatic lifestyle. The aquatic snake to arouse the most interest, however, is *Eunectes murinus*, the anaconda. Herpetologists are sceptical about some of the more outlandish claims made about this legendary animal, but authenticated measurements exist of almost seven metres, making the anaconda one of the world's largest snakes. Like the Old World pythons and the boa constrictors of the neotropics, anacondas are constricting predators. They lie in wait along riverbanks and in floating vegetation to ambush prey, which may include fish, turtles, wading birds, capybara, caiman and even animals as large as tapir, seizing the victim by the neck and rapidly throwing several coils around it. The snake's grip tightens progressively until struggling ceases, when it will often repair to the water with its meal for the lengthy process of ingestion. Anacondas are most often encountered as a series of brownish coils wrapped around the branches of a waterside tree.

The most dangerous Amazonian snakes are undoubtedly the Crotalinae or pit vipers, which include both the fer-de-lance *Bothrops atrox* and the magnificent bushmaster *Lachesis muta*. Lachesis, in classical mythology, spun the thread of human life: pit vipers are not to be trifled with. They are capable of delivering a large dose of powerful venom, guided by the 'pits' or heat sensory depressions

Visitors may see the lizard, *Kentropyx altamazonica*, even on the decks of floating houses.

The beautiful vine snake, *Oxybelis fulgidus*, (below, at left) can be observed in the trees.

The Amazonian fer-de-lance (*Bothrops atrox*) also climbs trees at high water. Be careful, it is a very poisonous snake!

The adult *Chironius scurrulus* snake (immature forms are green) is not aquatic, but it is often seen near the water.

The boa constrictor (*Boa constrictor*) is not poisonous, but like the anaconda, kills its victims (e.g., sloths and monkeys) by constriction.

The tamacuaré (*Uranoscodon superciliosus*) lizard sometimes climbs up in the trees, but it also runs on the surface of the water with incredible skill. Jacarerana (*Crocodilurus lacertinus*) means false caiman, and its habits are like those of the caiman.

The leaf toad *Bufo nasicus* (above), can be seen sleeping during the day, but tree frogs hide themselves very well.

Other creatures of the night: at left, frogs *Hyla punctata* (above) and *Scinax nebulosus*.

close to the eyes that help the snake to strike accurately. Pit vipers are largely terrestrial and rarely seen near Mamirauá, but a sensible caution should be shown with all snakes until they are properly identified.

Amphibians

Also venomous are some members of the Dendrobatidae family, also known as poison-dart frogs. The toxic secretions of a species occurring in Colombia are used by Indians to tip their hunting darts. They seem to fabricate their chemical defences from substances contained in stinging ants in their diet, and many species in this family use striking and beautiful colouration to advertise their unpalatability.

The member of this family to occur in Mamirauá, *Epipedobates hahneli*, is black with patches of yellow and blue on its back and belly. Unlike its cousins, *Epipedobates* is only mildly toxic, and spends most of the year on the forest floor, probably passing the floods on floating or emergent vegetation.

Amphibians are inextricably linked with water. As a group they lay eggs without protective shells, and their permeable skins must be kept moist to avoid desiccation and death. The humidity of tropical rainforest offers many advantages, therefore, and the watery world of the *várzea* would seem to offer even more.

In truth, however, there are few truly aquatic frogs or toads in the *várzea*, as the vast diversity of fish out-compete them for food and prey heavily on eggs and tadpoles deposited in the lakes and streams. Nonetheless, a diverse family of frogs, the Hylidae, have colonised the *capim* floating meadows, and an evening canoe trip past the rafts of grass reveals the extraordinary variety and volume of their songs.

Faced with heavy tadpole predation, some neotropical anurans have evolved innovative reproductive techniques to protect their offspring. The toad *Pipa pipa* is relatively large, at 17cm, and has an extraordinarily flattened body shape, an adaptation that, along with partially webbed feet, seems to suit its aquatic lifestyle.

Pipa copulation takes place in the water, with the male mounting the female and securing her with his front legs. From here the process becomes increasingly bizarre. The couple begin to swim in vertical circles, slowly ascending, and whilst looping the loop the female lays her eggs. These are fertilised and manoeuvred into position by the male, apparently assisted by their strange choreography, until all hundred or so eggs lie in the centre of the female's back. During the next 24 hours these will be encased in chambers of a spongy material that grows around them, until each egg is secured in its own cell. For a hundred days or so, the female will carry her developing brood around on her back, whilst they undergo all the immature stages of their life in this protected environment, until they are ready to break themselves loose and swim off on their own, miniature replicas of their parents.

VASCO

THE FISH OF MAMIRAUÁ

Paddling through Mamirauá at the height of the flood, you become aware of a world of activity in the submerged forest beneath your canoe. As ants and spiders crowd onto the last dry branches of the smaller trees, dark shapes patrol the water beneath them, and the unfortunate arthropods who lose their grip do not last long on the surface. The splash of falling fruit is quickly followed by another splash as an eager mouth pulls it under. And a series of ripples reveal the presence of predators on the hunt. The rising water level forces terrestrial animals to flee the floodplain or take to the trees, but for the fish of the *várzea* it opens up a rich environment, with a host of new feeding opportunities.

Not everyone can take advantage of them, however. Decaying leaves and organic matter on the now submerged forest floor strip the oxygen that fish need from the great sheet of water moving slowly through the *várzea*. Any fish that enters the flooded forest must have a strategy for surviving these 'hypoxic' conditions, and *várzea* fish have evolved a series of intriguing adaptations to cope. With an equally impressive range of feeding specialisations, this makes for one of the most diverse ichthyofaunas in the world. Research at Mamirauá has identified more than 350 species inhabiting or using the reserve at different stages of the flood cycle.

Parental care: the aruanã

These fish are the most important economic resource of the Amazon basin. The urban centres of the region depend on tens of thousands of tons of fish sold each year at their major fish markets: neither could exist without the flooded forest. Other fish less palatable to people represent the major food resource of a host of mammals, birds, reptiles and invertebrates. Predator pressure is intense, yet many fish use the várzea for reproduction. The wealth of nutrients it provides are necessary for some species to reach full sexual maturity, and its varied habitats offer food and

A fisherman proudly shows off a pacarari catfish (*Pseudoplatystoma tigrinum*).

Fish from Mamirauá arriving at the market in Tefé.

Three of the most important commercial fish from Mamirauá: aruanã (*Osteoglossum bicirrhosum*), tucunaré, or peacock bass (*Cichla ocellaris*) and tambaqui (*Colossoma macropomum*).

Gutting a tambaqui for supper at Boca do Mamirauá.

some measure of safety to their young. The *várzea* is a fish nursery, but a hazardous one. Some species have evolved complicated strategies to protect their brood.

Few parents can be as jealous of their offspring's welfare as the male aruanã *Osteoglossum bicirrhosum*. These strange, flattened fish reproduce as the floodwaters rise, and once the eggs are fertilised the male opens his large mouth and takes them in. Here the eggs hatch, and here the young fish develop for the next 2-3 weeks, until father lets them out for their first glimpse of the world beyond the parental teeth. Though they now begin to feed on algae and microscopic invertebrates, for the next month or so they remain close to the male aruanã, ready to retreat inside his mouth if danger threatens. The adult fish has long chin barbels, whose resemblance to the young fish may help to guide the brood toward their safe haven. They probably have some role as sensory appendages, and may also serve to gather precious oxygen as the fish cruise at the surface. The aruanã is an opportunist predator, and the retina of its eye is divided horizontally, an adaptation that allows the fish to search for prey both in and out of the water, spotting falling insects before they hit the surface and beating competitive fish to the prize.

Any object falling into the water in the flooded forest attracts the attention of shoals of other fish cruising just below the surface, perpetually on the lookout for insects, seeds and fruit dropping from the canopy above. Many of these fish, such as the frugivorous pacu *Mylossoma* spp., have a flattened profile that enables them to swim more effectively at the surface and take advantage of the thin layer of oxygen-rich water where air and water meet. But the sharp eyesight of the aruanã allows it to jump the queue: in a dramatic ploy that has earned it the nickname 'water monkey', it is capable of leaping over a metre out of the water to seize beetles and even birds from low branches.

Fruit and fish: the tambaqui

The iycthyofauna of the flooded forest is unique in the number of species that it contains which feed on fruit and seeds. Research at Mamirauá has shown that 80% of *várzea* trees are adapted for animal seed dispersal, generally by the production of some form of fleshy fruit. The majority of these trees are fruiting during the flood season, when they are surrounded by water, suggesting that in the *várzea* fish have in large part taken on the ecological role of dispersal agents filled elsewhere by birds and mammals. Many *várzea* fruits will float on the surface, in easy reach of a frugivorous fish, but the seeds within will sink when the pulp falls away or after passing through the digestive tract of an unwitting host, ready to germinate when the waters recede.

Plants that encase their seeds in hard shells are generally pursuing an alternative strategy of dispersal. Spruce's rubber tree *Hevea spruceana* has hit upon a novel technique: when mature the pods explode, scattering the large seeds several metres from the parent trees. Waiting for the splash is one the most effective and voracious of the *várzea* seed predators, the tambaqui *Colossoma macropomum*. An elegant mossy green colour and reaching a metre in length and thirty kilos in weight, an adult tambaqui spends most of the year in the river channels, visiting the flooded forest at high water, where a peculiar, moustache-like protrusion on the lower lip helps to channel water across its gills and thus utilise more of what oxygen is available at the surface. Behind the lip is a powerful set of horse-like molars capable of crushing the toughest of seed cases, and the fish feeds heavily on seeds and fruit whilst the floods last, building up huge reserves of fat. These reserves are meant for the lean months that follow the retreat of the waters from the forest, but they also serve to make it one of the most delicious table fish in the world. Roasted '*na brasa*' in the local manner, over an open fire, tambaqui is a *várzea* delicacy. Unfortunately, its popularity has led to substantial over-exploitation, although studies are in progress to evaluate the potential for farming this magnificent fish.

Electric fish

Away from the forest, on the edges of the lakes and along the channels, high water brings another important habitat, with the growth of the floating meadows. These are rafts of grasses and other herbaceous plants whose roots dangle free in the water and trap the nutrients they need from the load being borne past on the current. Rich in invertebrate life, the dark world underneath the meadows provides a promising environment for fish species that can navigate the complex tangle of roots. Gymnotiformes, or knife fish, as their name suggests, have blade-like bodies well suited to manoeuvring in this kind of substrate. But a slim profile alone is not enough: deprived of visual cues the knife fish need an alternative method of finding their way.

Many fish are sensitive to electricity, including sharks and several of the catfish species found in Mamirauá. The Gymnotiformes, also known as Amazon electric fish, take the process a stage further. Specialised electrocells, surrounded by insulating tissue and stimulated by nervous signals, generate a weak electric field around the fish. Using a network of electroreceptors along the body, electric fish can then detect fluctuations in this field caused by their surroundings, and in this way locate obstructions, prey objects and each other in the maze under the meadows. Each species employs a distinct signal, essential to avoid jamming, and the preliminary results of research under way at Mamirauá suggest that the nature of this signal has itself evolved to suit the particular environment of the individual species. Electric

Children gutting catfish:
pacamum, caparari
and piracatinga.

Electric fish from Mamirauá:
below, the elegant knife fish
(*Steatogenys elegans*),
and the electric eel
(*Electrophorus electricus*)
that can generate a charge of
up to 500 volts.

fish that live in fast moving water tend to have high frequency signals, allowing them to update their 'image' of their surroundings rapidly. Where detail is more important, in the sluggish water under the meadows, lower frequency signals are the norm.

The knife fish exhibit a range of adaptations to low oxygen conditions, and a related species, the electric eel *Electrophorus electricus*, gulps air at the surface, from which the oxygen is extracted via vascularized protuberances in its mouth. As its name suggests, the electric eel also has its own internal battery, though of a wholly different order. Whilst the knife fish produce fields of a few millivolts, Electrophorus can generate a discharge of up to five hundred volts, enough to stun its prey and give fishermen a nasty shock should they inadvertently bring one up in their nets.

Low water

With the withdrawal of the floodwaters from the forest in the months of August and September, conditions for the *várzea* fish change drastically. Species that have invaded the forest to feed during the high water period must now escape or risk being stranded in rapidly drying pools. This may not be the disaster it seems: some species, including the traíra *Hoplias malabaricus*, have evolved the ability to crawl out of shallow water and wriggle to better alternatives nearby. The odd, worm like lungfish *Lepidosiren paradoxa* can wait out the dry season in burrows in the mud, breathing with its lung and slowing its metabolic processes to conserve energy until the floods return.

But most species must retreat before the forest dries, and as the *várzea* lakes become cut off from the main river systems by the falling water levels, they fill with fish, and predators. Amongst the most visible are the piranhas, particularly the red-bellied piranha *Pygocentrus nattereri*, which reaches great concentrations in some *várzea* lakes at this time. These piranha hunt in packs, and are quickly drawn to any commotion in the water. Fishing for piranha at low water is gratifyingly simple, and dozens of little snapping fish can be hauled from the water in a matter of minutes. Care must be taken, however, when handling the catch, as piranhas display a formidable set of razor sharp teeth, quite capable of inflicting a serious wound, as the fingers of many fishermen attest. Local people, whose lives require them to be often in the water or be engaged in tasks, such as gutting fish at the river's edge, which attract the fish, demonstrate a healthy respect for the piranha, and many can show scars on their fingers or feet. The danger from these fish is often overstated, yet it is wise to take advice before jumping in, even on the hottest day, and especially at low water.

Top: Pirarucu, or arapaima (*Arapaima gigas*), is the largest scale fish in the Amazon.

Below, the piranha (*Pygocentrus nattereri*), a myth blown out of proportion by Hollywood, the spotted sting ray and the acará-bandeira, a beautiful aquarium fish.

Pirarucu

If fishing for piranha is the province of children and visitors, fishing for the pirarucu *Arapaima gigas*, most fascinating of the aquatic predators of Mamirauá and the symbol of the reserve, is strictly for the experts. The rewards for a successful hunt are considerable: pirarucu can reach three metres in length and a weight of two hundred kilos, making them one of the largest freshwater fish in the world. Joining battle in the traditional way, armed only with a steel-tipped harpoon in a flimsy canoe, calls on all the fisherman's reserves of skill, experience and courage. Able to breathe air via a modified swim bladder, the pirarucu is ideally adapted for life as a predator of the *várzea* lakes, where its prey is often rendered sluggish by the low oxygen levels. But this adaptation is also its undoing, as it must rise to the surface every fifteen minutes or so to take another gulp of air. The fisherman, alerted by ripples on the surface of the water or by small bubbles rising from the depths, is waiting. As the fish breaks surface, he strikes, hurling a two-metre harpoon from the prow of his canoe with enough strength to pierce the armoured scales of the fish with its barbed tip. When the struggle is over, the fisherman may have to sink his craft in the shallows in order to load the fish aboard and paddle for home.

The flesh is removed in great fillets or '*mantas*', which are traditionally salted to preserve them. Pirarucu is highly prized in the Amazon, and is often served at village celebrations or football matches. Commercialisation of the pirarucu fishery is nothing new, indeed at the end of the last century more than a thousand tons of fish were sold annually at market in Belém, the great port city at the mouth of the Amazon. Recently, however, spiralling demand from the urban centres of the region, together with the introduction of gill netting, has precipitated a drastic decline in pirarucu stocks. Constraints on the size of fish that may be landed and a complete ban on the fishery during the breeding season, from December until May, have been introduced, but the high prices that pirarucu can command mean these regulations are often ignored. The pirarucu makes an appropriate symbol for Mamirauá; perhaps more than any other species it embodies the challenge of sustainable management of the *várzea's* resources.

Seasonal visitors

To the resident fish fauna of the flooded forest must be added a group of visitors, residents of the deep rivers outside the reserve but attracted at low water into the *paranás* or channels that run through the *várzea*, which at this time of year offer well oxygenated water and abundant food. Important in the diet of local people and in commercial fishing are the large predatory catfish, including the surubim

Pseudoplatystoma fasciatum, which can reach a metre in length and displays a beautiful striped colouration in shades of grey. Following the catfish are a group of small but sinister fish that have a place in Amazonian mythology equal to that of the piranha. Fishermen hauling surubim from the river occasionally notice small fish about the size of a slim cigarette emerge from under the gill covers and slip wriggling into the water. These are the Trichomycteridae, one of several species to go by the local name candiru, and they live as parasites, sucking blood from the gills of their unfortunate hosts. They are also the origin of the oft-repeated admonition to the unwary Amazon explorer never to urinate in the water. Local people ignore this with impunity, and the visitor in need may follow suit with reasonable confidence.

More real hazard is presented by another low water visitor to the *várzea*, the freshwater stingrays. These fascinating and beautiful predators give credence to the hypothesis that the Amazon basin once drained westwards. Their nearest surviving cousins are found in the Pacific, and scientists now believe that the populations became isolated only when the rising Andes closed off the basin to the west and began the river's long progress eastwards. More practically, they are an excellent reason to avoid wading in the shallows along the sandy beaches that appear during the season of low water. Cryptic and fond of burying themselves in the sand, their sting is serrated and wickedly sharp, and injects a venom that can cause extreme pain in anyone unfortunate enough to step on them.

Aquarium fish

The enthusiasm of tropical fish hobbyists in Europe, the US and the Far East for the more spectacular Amazon species provides a large and growing market for these fish, and since the construction of the international airport at Manaus exports from the region have exploded. Estimates place the annual number of fish passing through the city at 20 million or so, though this probably underestimates the trade, as there are incentives for dealers to under-report and many fish die in transit.

Some of the most valuable aquarium fish come from the black water of the Rio Negro and tributaries, but the *várzea* is the home of the beautiful discus *Symphysodon aequifasciatus*, which occurs in Mamirauá in a blue form particularly sought after by collectors and dealers. The result has been the commercial extinction of the species within the reserve during a period of heavy exploitation at the beginning of the 1990's. Now protected, researchers expect the stocks to recover only slowly. Discus are highly selective in their choice of mate and their breeding is easily disturbed. Nevertheless, it may be possible to develop a sustainable programme for the exploitation of these beautiful and valuable fish.

INSECTS

Blue morpho butterfly or *mutuca* biting fly: insects dominate the *várzea*. Making up about 90% of the arthropods, or jointed invertebrates; whether the measure is diversity, biomass or sheer numbers, insects are the most successful class of animal in the flooded forest. Paradoxically, they are amongst the least studied. No one knows how many species of insect inhabit the Amazon basin, though it seems likely to run into millions. Though there are some strikingly large and colourful species, most insects are small and cryptic, and hard to study in the wild. Others are possessed of fierce bites and stings with which to reward the field biologist's attention. Relatively few of the life histories of *várzea* insects are well understood, but they are some of the most fascinating. *Várzea* plants and insects have evolved side by side, developing co-evolutionary relationships of mutual dependence and complexity.

Non-insect arthropods have also been successful in the flooded forest: the many species of spider include the large tarantulas or *caranguejeiras*, whose prey includes small mammals and birds. Of the crustaceans, three species of crab and four of shrimp occupy a crucial position in the food web of the *várzea* lakes and channels, being an important part of the diet of various fish and birds. At least one species, *Macrobrachium amazonicum*, the Amazon freshwater shrimp, is eaten by man. But this chapter will concentrate on the insects, and none are more prominent in *várzea* life than the ants and termites.

Leaf-cutter ants

Amongst the most numerous, and conspicuous, of the ants are the leaf cutters *Atta* spp. They form vast nests of up to 8m individuals, spread out over large areas with several entrances linked by tunnels, and range in size from the diminutive minima caste whose duties keep them inside the nest, to the 20mm soldiers on duty at the

A blue morpho butterfly *Morpho menelaus*, whose beautiful colour comes from the reflection and refraction of sunlight on its tiny scales, and the owl butterfly *Caligo illioneus*.

entrances. Most often seen, however, are the 10mm worker ants also known as foragers, who patrol the forest in search of suitable vegetation for cropping. The ants are quite choosy and seem to avoid plants with high concentrations of toxic chemicals. Once a promising tree or shrub has been located, the ants chew a semi-circular section in the leaf, grip it between their jaws and tear it off. The prize, which may be many times larger than the ant, is them borne off to the nest in determined if slightly awkward fashion, and the sight of hundreds of leaf fragments bumping and waving across the forest floor is one of the most peculiar and comic in the *várzea*. But there is nothing comic about the scale of their operations. Studies suggest that leaf cutter ants remove as much leaf material as all the vertebrate folivores combined, an estimated 15-20% of primary production.

What do the ants do with all those leaves? They don't eat them, although they do seem to taste the leaves and may suck some of the juices released. Ants cannot however digest the cellulose in leaves, as Bates knew. His solution, that the leaves were being used to thatch the chambers of the nest against heavy rainfall, was picturesque, but wrong.

In fact, the leaves are fodder, or perhaps more properly fertiliser, for the underground gardens that the ants diligently tend. In one of the most bizarre of the co-evolutionary relationships that characterise tropical forests, the nests of leaf cutter ants are home to a fungus that occurs nowhere else. The foragers deliver the cropped leaves to the gardener ants, which chew them up and mix them into a sticky mass with saliva and faecal material. This compost is then added to the existing beds, and a cutting from the fungus, a sort of spongy, bread like material, placed on it. Within a few days, the fungus has colonised the leaf matter, and the ants can harvest a meal from it.

When, periodically, the colony produces a new queen, she takes with her on her mating flight a precious fragment of the fungus in her mouth. Having mated in mid air with a male from another colony, she digs a narrow shaft about 10cm deep and there in a small chamber she begins her first garden. For a month or more she remains there without food or water, tending the fungus, feeding it with her eggs and faeces. If the fungus dies so will she, as she has no way of obtaining more. After this period, if the garden flourishes, the first worker ants will emerge and take over gardening duties, freeing the queen to set about reproduction in earnest.

Cecropia Ants

Cecropia or trumpet trees are typical of the low-lying areas of the *várzea*. They are amongst the quickest trees to colonise disturbed areas or new land being formed

The cecropia tree (*Cecropia* sp.) houses huge populations of cecropia ants *Azteca* sp. (detail).

by sediment deposition, and their strategy is speed, out-competing other species by getting more leaves higher quicker. They do not invest the energy other trees devote to chemical defences, and yet their tempting green leaves are ignored by all but a few of the many hungry herbivores of the *várzea*. To find out why, tap the stem, but be prepared for a rapid withdrawl. Like bamboo, *Cecropia* grows in hollow segments, and it has evolved a number of baits to tempt ants of the *Azteca* genus to take up residence within.

The first thing the *Cecropia* provides is a way in. A small section of the tree just below each node is unvascularized, and here the queen ant can chew her way in without becoming gummed up with sticky sap released if other parts of the tree are cut into. Once inside, she walls herself up and lays her eggs. The larvae feed on the pith inside the stem cavity, developing into worker *Azteca* who take over brood care and expand the accommodations, chewing through the conveniently thin septum or membrane into adjoining segments of the tree and killing or walling up any other queens that may have entered, until the whole tree is colonised. Attention then turns to the exterior of the *Cecropia*, where the velvety hairs on the underside of the leaves facilitate ant locomotion. A nutritious oil is extracted from other leaf hairs, whilst energy-rich swellings at the base of the stems, known as 'extra-floral nectaries', are also harvested.

The advantages of life in the *Cecropia* for the ant are plain. But what does the ant-plant get from the relationship? The obvious and dramatic one is defence. Shake a *Cecropia* branch and immediately it swarms with *Azteca*. The fierce stinging ants drive off almost all leaf predators from the tree. They also cut away any vines that attempt to coil themselves around it and even destroy nearby plants that might compete for light with the host. More subtly, they may well contribute to the plant's nutrition. In their foraging, *Azteca* ants bring back organic matter to the tree, which is eventually deposited, together with faecal matter and ant corpses, in colony dumps. This 'ant compost' can then be reabsorbed by the host, providing a valuable source of nutrition in poor soil.

Fig wasps

Apart from ants the Hymenoptera order of social insects also includes the wasps and bees, of which the *várzea* is home to several species, often quite formidably large. But perhaps the most extraordinary is a tiny wasp, which plays a role out of proportion to its size in the life cycle of another landmark *várzea* tree. The peculiar habits of the fig *Ficus* spp. have been discussed elsewhere in this book, and its abundant fruits provide food for many *várzea* species. But before the fig feast can take place, fig wasps from the family Agaonidae, no larger than the head of a match, have to play their part. Figs occur around the world, and each species has a species of wasp to pollinate it. Without pollination, the seeds of the fig are not viable, and the fruit will not ripen.

The immature fruit, or syconia, of the fig are peculiar in that they contain hundreds of miniature florets with fully formed and receptive stigma. Female fig wasps arrive at the small, hard fruit and squeeze through a tiny opening in the end. In the process their wings are torn off: they will not leave the fig again. Once inside, the female wasp makes a tour of the florets, laying an egg in each one and in the process pollinating the fruit. Parasitic wasps may also enter and lay eggs without pollinating, but at least one agaonid must arrive for the fruit to be viable. Once her egg laying is complete, she dies in the fruit.

A month later, the male fig wasps emerge and immediately burrow into the tightly packed florets, cutting holes and inserting their abdomens to mate with the unborn females. They may fight to death with each other for access to the females at this stage. Within two days, the mated females will themselves emerge, helped out of the florets by the males, who now put aside their differences to try to cut a passage out of the fruit. Meanwhile the females tour the male florets and fill their thorax pockets with pollen. The fruit wall breached, the males fall dead to the forest floor, and the females follow them out, in search of a new fig tree. Behind them, the fruit ripens, to be eaten later by bird or monkey, oblivious to the drama that preceded its meal.

Butterflies and moths

Of the other flying insects, the most prominent are the Lepidoptera, the moths and butterflies, *mariposas* and *borboletas* in Portuguese. Perhaps the most striking amongst the latter are the giant butterflies of the subfamily Morphinae, the males of which display stunning iridescent blue colouration, the product of the refraction of light in miniature translucent scales in the wings. Two species, *Morpho achilles* and *M. menelaus*, have been recorded in Mamirauá, and they can be seen in heavy flight along *várzea* trails. Their colouring is a means of communication between butterflies, and Morphos can be attracted to any blue and shiny object.

Another large and dramatic Mamirauá butterfly is *Caligo illioneus*, from a broadly distributed genus also known as the owl butterflies, after the large and conspicuous 'owl eyes' on the underside of the hind wings. Lepidopterists agree that these markings must protect the butterfly from predation in some way, but the precise mechanism is contested. One theory is that display of the eye spots when threatened mimics a large vertebrate and deters the potential predators; another holds that the spots form misleading targets for determined predators, diverting the attack to a non-essential portion of the butterfly and enabling escape with only superficial damage. *Caligo* does not visit flowers but feeds instead on rotting fruit and secretions exuded from trees attacked by wood boring insects. This diet is not unusual in neo-tropical butterflies, and is followed by *Hamadryas feronia*, a species hard to spot at rest, perched head downwards on a tree trunk with its cryptically coloured wings outstretched. On the wing, however, it draws attention to itself by a strange crackling sound that gives it its common name of 'click' or 'cracker' butterfly. The purpose of this sound is not understood, though it may be linked to courtship display or the territories of the males.

One of the best-studied groups of neo-tropical butterflies is the nectivorous Heliconiinae, of which four species have been recorded in Mamirauá. Sometimes called 'long wings', Heliconids are beautiful and graceful butterflies, often seen in lazy and conspicuous flight along trails and in the 'light gaps' where canopy trees have fallen. Adults of the same species have the strange habit for a butterfly of returning every night to roost together in the thin branches of the sub-canopy. Although the focus of much scientific attention, this behaviour remains poorly understood. Evolutionary biologists are interested in the ongoing tussle between the butterfly and the vine that plays unwilling host to hungry Heliconid caterpillars, the *Passiflora* or passionflower. The conventional chemical defences of the vine have been largely neutralised by the caterpillars, which take up or sequester the toxic compounds in the leaves to provide themselves and the adult butterflies that they will become with added protection from predators. Heliconids advertise their unpalatability with distinctive markings, which form the basis of an extensive mimicry complex, as other non toxic species derive advantage from adopting the same colouration. The passionflower has escalated the conflict by developing special organs, known as extra-floral nectaries, to attract aggressive insects such as ants and wasps, which then attack the Heliconid caterpillars. It has been suggested that some species of vine develop small yellow spots that resemble Heliconid eggs, to the extent that female butterflies are deceived into avoiding these vines in their search for an unoccupied passionflower leaf.

Greeny-yellow or orange butterflies from the families Pieridae and Papilionidae also form large agglomerations. Males of the genus *Phoebis* spp., the sulphur butterflies, swarm in huge numbers on the wet sand of the *várzea* beaches as the floods recede, but will also come to puddles or to fresh urine, which can be surprising if you step off the trail to answer a call of nature. The butterflies greedily suck

A long-winged *Heliconius wallacei* sucking nectar from a passion flower (*Passiflora coccinea*) and two *Heliconius antiochus* in the "dormitory".

Paulograma peristera, a relative of the 88 butterflies.
Below: *Hamadryas feronia*, the click butterfly, perched head downwards.

A *panapaná* (gathering) of pierid butterflies.

up the mineral salts, possibly for their nutritional value, or more likely as a precursor for the synthesis in their bodies of mating pheromones. Adult *Phoebis* are fast fliers and habituate open areas, where they visit flowers for nectar.

To appreciate the variety and beauty of the moths of the *várzea*, a night expedition is required. Whilst flowers that are adapted to attract day-flying butterflies are often brightly coloured, moth pollinated plants tend to produce white blooms which open at night when the moths are active, and which give off a powerful gardenia-like fragrance. A major food resource for the bat populations, moths have evolved their own countermeasures in this night-time arms race, including the ability to detect the bat's echolocation and even make jamming signals of their own to confuse the predator. Some moths are diurnal, often using bright colours of their own to imitate wasps or inedible butterflies.

One of the spectacular species of Sphingidae, or sphinx moths, found in Mamirauá is *Pseudosphinx tetrio*, sometimes known as the Frangipani Sphinx, after the fragrant trees on which its caterpillars feed. In the *várzea*, the caterpillars are found on *Himatanthus attenuata*, the sucuúba tree. Unlike most moth caterpillars, *Pseudosphinx* are highly conspicuous, an eye catching black with bright yellow rings and a red-orange head. This colour pattern warns predators that the caterpillar is inedible, due to the highly toxic substances in the plant on which it feeds. As adults, sphinx moths are capable of aerobatic feats: they can fly backwards and hover in front of a flower to feed in a high wind. Large and streamlined insects, they have been shown to travel several kilometres during a night's foraging, and are thus pollinators of many *várzea* plants.

Greater travellers still, the population explosions and subsequent migrations of the *Urania leilus* moth have been observed and recorded since the nineteenth century. These diurnal moths are black with iridescent green on the wings, and resemble swallowtail butterflies in their graceful shape. The species occurring in Mamirauá is *U. leilus*, though closely related species are found in Central America, Cuba and Jamaica, following the distribution of *Omphalea* spp., a forest liana on which the moths lay their eggs. *U. leilus* is a migratory species and in some years huge numbers of moths can be seen crossing the Amazon, often pausing on the boats headed up or down the river. The reason behind these migrations still evades lepidopterists, though there may be some connection with a build up of toxicity in the host plant.

Beetles

Coleoptera, insects with hard wing cases or elytra, are perhaps the most diverse of all the insect orders. Amongst the bewildering variety of beetles are some so

Above: *Rothschildia erycina* moths mating while the female eclodes from the cocoon.
Diurnal moth, *Urania leilus*, sucking up water from the ground.

Below, a master of disguise: a ctenuchid moth that mimics wasps.
A saturnid moth opening its wings to show the ocelli that scare away possible predators – the photographer in this case.

A non-insect arthropod: a tarantula from Mamirauá, which visitors will certainly see on the tree trunks.

The harlequin beetle (*Acrocinus longimanus*) and, at right, the rhinoceros beetle (*Megasoma gyas*) are two of the most spectacular insects in the Amazon.

When the crepuscular dragonflies come out at Mamirauá, it is time for visitors to go in. They are effective predators of mosquitoes, which they hunt at dusk. But this photo shows a diurnal species.

striking that they make their way into handicrafts. The Buprestidae or wood-boring beetles are also known as jewel beetles for their beautifully coloured wing cases, used by Amerindians as ornaments.

Male rhinoceros beetles *Megasoma* spp. develop massive antlers. They are amongst the largest *várzea* beetles, up to 8cm in length, and truly impressive animals.

Less prepossessing beetles from the family Scarabaeidae have a crucial role in the annual flowering of the *Victoria amazonica*, the giant water lily. The plants flower at the height of the floods, and many hundreds of white blooms may open simultaneously at dusk on the lakes of Mamirauá. As they open, the internal temperature of the flowers rises by more than ten degrees, and a strong scent is emitted, which along with the white colour of the petals attracts the scarab beetle *Cyclocephala* spp. The beetles spend the night in the flowers and are trapped inside when promptly at dawn the petals close. They pass the day feeding on a starchy material provided by the flower, triggering the release of pollen with which the beetles become thoroughly smeared as they move around the flower. At dusk, when the flower opens for the second and final time, the beetles leave with their pollen load, in search of another flower. The petals have now turned red and the scent has gone, so no new scarabs arrive. Instead the flower sinks slowly to the bottom of the lake, where the seed will mature before floating to the surface to be dispersed by the currents.

Dragonflies and mosquitoes

Sitting outside at the floating house and enjoying the sunset, the visitor to Mamirauá will be struck by the arrival of the crepuscular dragonflies, suddenly and with a precision you could set your watch by. Dragonflies and damselflies of the order Odonata are handsome and impressive aerial predators, but their arrival is a sign to head indoors, as their prey in many cases are the several species of mosquito that become active with the dusk.

There are about 3000 species of mosquito in the world, of which 30% or so live in the neotropics. All need water of some kind to breed, and the *várzea* offers many such habitats, from the lakes and waterways themselves to the tiny containers provided by bromeliads and tree holes. Local people in Mamirauá without the benefit of screened accommodation eat dinner early, to be under their nets before the first wave of mosquitoes arrive, shortly after dusk. There is then usually a lull, before another peak just before dawn. Overnight fishing expeditions, though necessary at certain times of the year, are not a popular detail.

REFERENCES

AURICCHIO, Paulo. *Primatas do Brasil.* São Paulo: Terra Brasilis, 1995.

AYRES, J. M. Comparative feeding ecology of the Uakari and Bearded Saki, *Cacajao* and *Chiropotes*. *Journal of Human Evolution*, 1989.

———. *On a New Species of Squirrel Monkey, Genus Saimiri, from Brazilian Amazonia.* Papéis Avulsos de Zoologia. São Paulo: USP, 1985.

———. *As matas de várzea do Mamirauá.* Brasília, DF: Sociedade Civil Mamirauá, 1995.

BATES, Henry Walter. *The Naturalist on the Amazons*. London: John Murray, 1863.

EMMONS, Louise H. & FEER, François. *Neotropical Rainforest Mammals*: a field guide. Chicago: University of Chicago Press, 1990.

FORSHAW, Joseph M. *Parrots of the World.* Melbourne: Lansdowne Editions, 1989.

GOULDING, Michael. *Amazon*: the flooded forest. London: BBC Books, 1989.

GOULDING, Michael, SMITH, Nigel J. H. & MAHAR, Dennis J. *Floods of Fortune*: ecology and economy along the Amazon. Columbia: Columbia University Press, 1996.

KRICHER, John C. *A Neotropical Companion.* Princeton: Princeton University Press, 1997.

MITCHELL, Andrew W. *The Enchanted Canopy*. London: Collins, 1986.

MONTEIRO, Salvador. *Amazonia Flora & Fauna.* Rio de Janeiro: Livroarte Editora, 1993.

OTERO, Luiz Soledade. *Borboletas*: beleza e comportamento de espécies brasileiras. Rio de Janeiro: Marigo Comunicação Visual, 1990.

PADOCH, C., AYRES, J. M., PINEDO-VASQUEZ, M. & HENDERSON, A. (Ed.) *Várzea*: diversity, development and conservation of Amazonia's whitewater floodplains. New York: The New York Botanical Garden Press. Proceedings of Macapá conference (12-14 December 1994), 1999.

PRANCE, Ghillean T. & LOVEJOY, Thomas E. (Ed.). *Key Environments*: Amazonia. IUCN and Pergamon Press, 1985.

QUEIROZ, Helder L. *Preguiças e guaribas*: os mamíferos folívoros arborícolas do Mamirauá. Brasília, DF: Sociedade Civil Mamirauá, 1995.

REYNOLDS, John E. III & ODELL, Daniel K. *Manatees and Dugongs.* Facts on File, 1991.

RIBEIRO, Berta G. *Amazônia urgente.* Publisher's National Union, 1992.

RIDGELY, Robert S. *The Birds of South America.* Oxford: Oxford University Press, 1989.

RIDGWAY, Sam & HARRISON, Sir Richard. *Handbook of Marine Mammals.* Volume 4: *River Dolphins and the Larger Toothed Whales.* Academic Press, 1989.

RIZZINI, C. T., COIMBRA FILHO, A. F. & HOUAISS, A. *Ecossistemas brasileiros*. Rio de Janeiro: Editora Index, 1988.

SNOW, David W. *The Cotingas.* Cornell: Cornell University Press, 1982.

SOCIEDADE Civil Mamirauá. *Mamirauá Management Plan*. Brasília, DF, 1996.

WALLACE, Alfred Russell. *Travels on the Amazon*. London: Ward, Lock & Co, 1853.

WOLFGANG, J. Junk (Ed.). *The Central Amazon Floodplain*: ecology of a pulsing system. Ecological Studies 126. Springer. 525 p., 1997.

APPENDIX

1- ECOTOURISM IN MAMIRAUÁ

What is ecotourism in Mamirauá?

In its zoning system, the Mamirauá Reserve management plan designated a special zone for the development of an ecotourism program, to exploit the scenic beauty of this protected area. The Mamirauá ecotourism program was developed as one of the strategies to ensure the future funding of the Mamirauá Institute, as well as a source of alternative income to local residents.

Mamirauá is a special place and a unique experience. It is a paradise for people who are fascinated by nature and wish to participate in a true ecotourism experience – one which counts on the participation of local communities, as well as its location in a pristine natural area.

The Reserve is one of the best places to view the rich Amazon wildlife. Besides the white uakari, endemic to the area, animals like howler monkeys, brown capuchin and squirrel monkeys, caimans, sloths and river dolphins are easily sighted on outings and excursions.

Furthermore, the Mamirauá Institute is developing several research projects, which ensure up-to-date information on the ecosystem and its species and even the possibility to interact with researchers.

Visitors leave knowing that their visit has contributed to the continuity of this important conservation work, which is serving as a replicable model to other conservation units around the globe.

Access

Tefé, the gateway to Mamirauá, is located 450km west of Manaus, and is not difficult to reach. You can travel to Tefé by boat or plane. There are scheduled Varig flights three times a week, as well as other regional airlines.

Once in Tefé there is a one and a half-hour trip on a speedboat to the Uakari Floating Lodge in Mamirauá.

The program

Arrival

Upon arrival at the Uakari Lodge, the visitor will be met by a bilingual field co-ordinator that will be present during your entire stay. If there is still daylight, you will then have the opportunity to go on a short exploratory canoe trip along the channels and lakes and maybe spot some nocturnal wildlife as you make your way home at dusk.

When you return to the floating house your dinner will be served. After dinner, if you are not too tired from your trip we recommend you watch a video, which will explain what the Mamirauá Institute is, how it was conceived, who are the partners of this conservation project and how it is divided. If you wish for further explanation, your host will be prepared to give you more information and reading material. At this point you should start thinking about whether you would like to pay a visit to a local community or not, so we can inform the village.

Second day

Our days at the lodge are planned to give you as much wildlife viewing opportunities as possible. The day starts early in Mamirauá and the animals wake up at dawn. Get ready to go on a walk in one of the trails specially prepared to see wildlife. Our trails are designed not to be physically straining and most of them can be walked in three hours at the longest. If you wish to help with the monitoring of the impact of theses trails on fauna, you will be given a form which you need to fill in some information, like whether you have seen the white uakari (*Cacajao calvus calvus*) and at what time.

All outings have to be accompanied by a guide, and you must listen to the guide's recommendation at all times, especially those regarding your own safety.

In the middle of the day, animal activity will be low. So after lunch you will have time to rest, read a book or watch the river flow by from a hammock. You can also select a video from our collection or just chat – outings will only be carried out when the sun goes down a little.

At around 3 o'clock you can start getting ready to go out. This time you will be taken on a motorised canoe to Lake Mamirauá. You will stay there until the sun sets and on your way back you will try and spot nocturnal fauna.

Researchers sometimes stop by the lodge and you may have the opportunity to have an informal chat about their work. Remember also that your host is always happy to discuss your impressions and findings of the day.

Third day

You will go on another trail this time, still with your guide, and you will now be a little more used to the forest. If you are really quiet, and set out early enough you might see even more wildlife, like capuchin monkeys, howlers, uakaris and squirrel monkeys, three toed sloths, hoatzins, etc.

If you chose to visit a local village, this afternoon is a good time to do it. You need to set out earlier than the day before because the villages are a little further. The ecotourism program has had plenty of discussion with the local communities about those visits and the villagers have established an informal itinerary with a series of things they would like to show you and talk about. The villager responsible for these visits will meet your group and show you around the village. You might have the opportunity to buy locally produced handicrafts, so take some small change with you.

After the visit you will go back to the floating house and will view wildlife on the way, finishing your trip watching the sunset again.

Fourth day

As it is your last day you will go on a trail and visit a lake or go out for traditional fishing. Your leaving time will depend on the time of your flight or boat.

As you leave please fill in our evaluation form. It is very important to us to know what you thought about the trip; this way we can always improve our services.

Hope you enjoy your stay.

THE MAMIRAUÁ ECOTOURISM PROGRAM

RECOMMENDATIONS

The rainforest is full of surprises, but a rainstorm is not one of those, please remember to bring rainproof clothes and shoes. Also be prepared for the mosquitoes in the jungle, there are more mosquitoes in the Solimões white water ecosystem than in the black water Rio Negro area, so don't forget insect repellent.

There is also much life underwater, including the presence of piranhas and venomous snakes. Thus we do not recommend the visitors to go into the water for a swim.

The outings to the lakes and channels will use motor-powered canoes. Make sure you are always wearing a life-saving jacket. Also, at these times it is essential to protect yourself from the tropical sun. We recommend high factor sun lotion and hats.

On these outings a guide will always accompany you and for your own safety it is not allowed to undertake excursions into the forest on your own.

The program offers an opportunity to interact with local people visiting a nearby village. When in contact with local inhabitants it is important to note that their culture and way of life are different. Please show respect to the traditional folk by always asking permission before taking any pictures.

During your visit to Mamirauá, remember that you are visiting a protected area; please do not remove any kind of biological material from the Reserve.

Contact address

Ecotourism Programme - Sociedade Civil Mamirauá
CP 38 - CEP 69470-000 - Tefé - Amazonas - Brazil
Phone/fax: + 55 (92) 343-4160

Reservations can be arranged with your agent
or by contacting ecomami@pop-tefe.rnp.br
Home page: www.mamiraua.org.br

2- FLORA SPECIES OF MAMIRAUÁ

FAMILY	SPECIES NAME	LOCAL NAMES
ANGIOSPERMAE		
Dicotiledonae		
Acanthaceae	*Justicia* aff. *laevilinguis*	-
Acanthaceae	*Justicia lindemani*	-
Acanthaceae	*Justicia pectoralis*	-
Acanthaceae	*Ruellia geminiflora*	-
Amaranthaceae	*Achyranthes* sp.	-
Amaranthaceae	*Alternanthera paronychoides*	-
Amaranthaceae	*Amaranthus luridus*	-
Amaranthaceae	*Celosia argentea*	-
Amaranthaceae	*Chamissoa altissima*	-
Amaranthaceae	*Pfaffia bracheata* ou *Iresine*	-
Anacardiaceae	*Anacardium occidentale**	caju
Anacardiaceae	*Spondias mombin*	taperebá
Annonaceae	*Annona* aff. *tenuipes*	boieira
Annonaceae	*Annona ambotaya*	biribá
Annonaceae	*Annona densicome*	araticum
Annonaceae	*Annona muricata**	graviola
Annonaceae	*Annona* sp.	envira-preta
Annonaceae	*Duguetia* cf. *marcgraviana*	envira-surucucu
Annonaceae	*Duguetia* cf. *spruceana*	envira-tracajá
Annonaceae	*Duguetia quitarensis*	envira-surucucu
Annonaceae	*Duguetia* sp.	envira-ferro
Annonaceae	*Guatteria dielsiana*	envira-fofa, envira-preta
Annonaceae	*Guatteria inundata*	envira-taia
Annonaceae	*Guatteria longicuspis*	envira-taia
Annonaceae	*Guatteria pteropus*	envira-fofa, envira-preta
Annonaceae	*Guatteria* sp. 1	envira, envira-de-folha-larga
Annonaceae	*Guatteria* sp. 2	envira
Annonaceae	*Guatteriopsis* cf. *kuhlmannii*	envira-vermelha
Annonaceae	*Guatteriopsis* sp.	envira-fofa, envira-tracajá
Annonaceae	*Oxandra polyantha*	envira, envira-preta, envirarana
Annonaceae	*Oxandra riedeliana*	envira-preta
Annonaceae	*Pseudoxandra polyphleba*	envira-preta, envira-amarela
Annonaceae	*Rollinia cuspidata*	envira
Annonaceae	*Rollinia mucosa*	biribá
Annonaceae	*Rollinia* sp.	biribá, biribazinho
Annonaceae	*Unonopsis lindmanii*	envira-preta, envira-branca
Annonaceae	*Unonopsis guatterioides*	cupiúba, envira-preta
Annonaceae	*Unonopsis* sp.	envira-de-folha-larga, envira-fofa
Annonaceae	*Xylopia calophylla*	envira-vassourinha
Annonaceae	*Xylopia* cf. *calophyllum*	envira-vassourinha
Annonaceae	*Xylopia* cf. *frutescens*	envira-vassourinha
Annonaceae	*Xylopia emarginata*	envira-vassourinha
Apocynaceae	*Aspidosperma excelsum*	carapanaúba
Apocynaceae	*Aspidosperma* sp.	carapanaúba

FAMILY	SPECIES NAME	LOCAL NAMES
Apocynaceae	*Himatanthus attenuata*	sucuúba
Apocynaceae	*Himatanthus tarapotensis*	sucuúba
Apocynaceae	*Malouetia* cf. *tamaquarina*	molongó
Apocynaceae	*Mandevilla* sp.	-
Apocynaceae	*Não identificada*	sorvarana
Apocynaceae	*Prestonia* sp.	-
Apocynaceae	*Rhabdodenia macrostoma*	-
Apocynaceae	*Tabernaemontana angulata*	-
Asclepiadaceae	*Ditassa aristata*	-
Asclepiadaceae	*Funastrum dombeyanum*	-
Asteraceae	*Acmella ciliata*	jamboa
Asteraceae	*Artemisia vulgaris*	cibalena, cibalena-planta
Asteraceae	*Ayapana triplinervis*	ajapana
Asteraceae	*Calyptocarpus biaristatus*	-
Asteraceae	*Eclipta prostrata*	-
Asteraceae	*Egletes viscosa*	-
Asteraceae	*Epaltes brasiliensis*	marcela
Asteraceae	*Erechtites heiracifolia*	-
Asteraceae	*Gymnocoronis spilanthoides*	-
Asteraceae	*Melanthera latifolia*	-
Asteraceae	*Mikania* sp.	-
Asteraceae	*Spilanthes acmella*	jambu
Bignoniaceae	*Crescentia cujete*	cuia
Bignoniaceae	*Memora* sp.	cipó
Bignoniaceae	*Pachyptera* sp.	cipó
Bignoniaceae	*Tabebuia barbata*	capitari
Bignoniaceae	*Tabebuia ochracea*	cipó
Bignoniaceae	*Tabebuia* sp.	capitari
Bignoniaceae	*Thynanthus panurensis**	cipó-alho
Bixaceae	*Bixa orellana**	urucu
Bombacaceae	*Ceiba pentandra*	samaúma, sumaúma
Bombacaceae	*Pachira aquatica*	mungubarana
Bombacaceae	*Pachira* cf. *insignis*	mungubarana
Bombacaceae	*Pseudobombax munguba*	munguba
Bombacaceae	*Quararibea cordata**	sapota
Bombacaceae	*Quararibea guianensis*	envira-de-urubu, pau-de-macaco
Boraginaceae	*Cordia* aff. *tetandra*	uruazeiro
Boraginaceae	*Cordia nodosa*	uruazeiro
Boraginaceae	*Cordia* sp.	louro-babão
Boraginaceae	*Heliotropum indicum*	-
Boraginaceae	*Heliotropum lagoense*	-
Boraginaceae	*Tournefortia laevigata*	-
Burseraceae	*Protium* sp.	breu
Caesalpiniaceae	*Bahuinia* sp.	-
Caesalpiniaceae	*Campsiandra angustifolia*	ingá-acapurana, acapurana-do-igapó, acapurana
Caesalpiniaceae	*Campsiandra comosa* var. *laurifolia*	acapurana
Caesalpiniaceae	*Cassia leiandra*	mari-mari
Caesalpiniaceae	*Copaifera* sp.	copaíba
Caesalpiniaceae	*Crudia amazonica*	orelha-de-cachorro, rim-de-paca, anaxi
Caesalpiniaceae	*Cynometra bauhinaefolia*	jutairana-preta, copaibarana, ripeira

FAMILY	SPECIES NAME	LOCAL NAMES
Caesalpiniaceae	*Cynometra marginata*	ripeira
Caesalpiniaceae	*Macrolobium acaciaefolium*	arapari
Caesalpiniaceae	*Macrolobium angustifolium*	arapari, arapari-orelha-de-macaco
Caesalpiniaceae	*Macrolobium bifolium*	araparirana
Caesalpiniaceae	*Macrolobium pendulum*	cedro-macho
Caesalpiniaceae	*Schizolobium parahybum*	-
Caesalpiniaceae	*Sclerolobium hypoleucon*	tachi
Caesalpiniaceae	*Senna obtusifolia*	-
Caesalpiniaceae	*Senna reticulata*	mata-pasto
Caesalpiniaceae	*Swartzia* aff. *leptopetala*	guajará
Capparidaceae	*Cleome parviflora*	-
Capparidaceae	*Cleome* sp.	-
Capparidaceae	*Crataeva benthamii*	cataurê, catoré, cipó-catoré-do-igapó
Capparidaceae	*Crataeva tapia*	cipó-catoré
Caprifoliaceae	*Sambucu nigra**	sabugueira
Caricacaea	*Carica papaya*	mamão
Caryocaraceae	*Caryocar microcarpum*	piquiarana, piquiá-bravo
Cecropiaceae	*Cecropia latiloba*	embaúba, imbaúba
Cecropiaceae	*Cecropia membranacea*	embaúba, imbaúba
Cecropiaceae	*Cecropia* sp.	-
Cecropiaceae	*Coussapoa asperifolia*	apuí
Cecropiaceae	*Coussapoa magnifolia*	apuí
Cecropiaceae	*Coussapoa nitida*	apuí, apuí-de-folha-larga
Cecropiaceae	*Coussapoa* spp.	apuí-folha-grande, apuí-pequeno
Cecropiaceae	*Pourouma* sp.	embaúba, embaubarana, imbaubarana
Celastraceae	*Hippocratea volubilis*	-
Celastraceae	*Maytenus guianensis*	muruxirana, muruxi-da-restinga, xixuá
Chenopodiaceae	*Chenopodium ambrosioides**	mastruz
Chrysobalanaceae	*Couclya* sp.	marirana
Chrysobalanaceae	*Couepia paraensis*	uixirana, pajurá-branco, macucurana, caraipé
Chrysobalanaceae	*Couepia subcordata*	marirana
Chrysobalanaceae	*Couepia ulei*	marirana, uixirana
Chrysobalanaceae	*Hirtella* sp. 1	-
Chrysobalanaceae	*Hirtella* sp. 2	macucurana
Chrysobalanaceae	*Licania apetala*	caraiperana-folha-lisa
Chrysobalanaceae	*Licania* cf. *canescens*	caraipé
Chrysobalanaceae	*Licania heteromorpha*	macucu-de-sangue, macucuí, abiorana, macucurana, macucu
Chrysobalanaceae	*Licania mollis*	caraiperana-folha-peluda
Chrysobalanaceae	*Licania parviflora*	caraipé
Chrysobalanaceae	*Licania* sp.	caraipé, caraiperana, macucurana
Chrysobalanaceae	*Parinari excelsa*	isqueira
Combretaceae	*Buchenavia macrophylla*	tanimbuca-folha-grande
Combretaceae	*Buchenavia ochroprumna*	tanimbuca
Combretaceae	*Buchenavia oxycarpa*	tanimbuca-folha-média
Combretaceae	*Buchenavia viridiflora*	tanimbuca-de-folha-miúda
Combretaceae	*Combretum rotundifolium*	escova-de-macaco
Combretaceae	*Combretum* sp.	pente-de-macaco
Combretaceae	*Terminalia dichotoma*	tanimbuca
Combretaceae	*Terminalia guianensis*	tanimbuca
Combretaceae	*Terminalia* sp.	tanimbuca

FAMILY	SPECIES NAME	LOCAL NAMES
Connaraceae	*Rourea camptoneura*	cipó
Convolvulaceae	*Dicranostyles ampla*	cipó-do-igapó, erva-de-passarinho
Convolvulaceae	*Ipomaea angulata*	-
Convolvulaceae	*Ipomaea aquatica*	-
Convolvulaceae	*Ipomaea phyllomega*	-
Convolvulaceae	*Ipomaea* sp.	-
Convolvulaceae	*Ipomaea squamata*	-
Cucurbitaceae	*Citrullus lanatus*	melancia
Cucurbitaceae	*Gurania bignonacea*	-
Cucurbitaceae	*Gurania* sp.	-
Cucurbitaceae	*Gurania spruceana*	-
Cucurbitaceae	*Luffia opercularis*	-
Cucurbitaceae	*Momordica charantia*	melão-são-caetano
Cucurbitaceae	*Rhytidostilis amazonica*	-
Dichapetalaceae	*Tapura amazonica*	morrão
Dilleniaceae	*Davilla* spp.	cipó-de-fogo
Dilleniaceae	*Não identificada*	caimbé
Ebenaceae	*Diospyros poeppigiana*	ripeira, caqui-preto
Ebenaceae	*Diospyros* sp.	pau-peludo, caqui
Elaeocarpaceae	*Sloanea gorkeana*	urucurana
Elaeocarpaceae	*Sloanea guianensis*	urucurana
Elaeocarpaceae	*Sloanea porphyrocarpa*	urucurana
Elaeocarpaceae	*Sloanea* sp.	urucurana-da-restinga
Elaeocarpaceae	*Sloanea ternifolia*	urucurana
Erythroxylaceae	*Erythroxylum anguifugum*	padozinho-vermelho
Erythroxylaceae	*Erythroxylum* sp.	caraiperana
Euphorbiaceae	*Acalypha acuminata*	-
Euphorbiaceae	*Alchornea castanaeifolia*	auerana, oirana
Euphorbiaceae	*Alchornea discolor*	supiarana, supiarana-do-igapó
Euphorbiaceae	*Alchornea fluviatilis*	supiarana
Euphorbiaceae	*Alchornea* sp.	supiarana-do-igapó
Euphorbiaceae	*Amanoa oblongifolia*	macucu-branco, macucu-de-casca-fina, macucurana, seringaí
Euphorbiaceae	*Caperonia latifolia* agg.	-
Euphorbiaceae	*Chamaesyce hyssopifolia*	-
Euphorbiaceae	*Croton cuneatus*	caferana
Euphorbiaceae	*Croton* sp.	pau-de-sangue
Euphorbiaceae	*Croton trinitatis*	-
Euphorbiaceae	*Croton urucurana*	-
Euphorbiaceae	*Discocarpus essequiboensis*	acapu-de-juruti
Euphorbiaceae	*Discocarpus* sp.	mututi
Euphorbiaceae	*Discocarpus spruceanus*	acapu-de-juruti
Euphorbiaceae	*Drypetes amazonica*	mané-corninho
Euphorbiaceae	*Drypetes variabilis*	capinuri, mané-corninho
Euphorbiaceae	*Euphorbia prostrata*	-
Euphorbiaceae	*Glycydendron amazonicum*	supiarana, catoré-branco
Euphorbiaceae	*Hevea brasiliensis*	seringueira
Euphorbiaceae	*Hevea spruceana*	seringa-barriguda
Euphorbiaceae	*Hura crepitans*	açacu
Euphorbiaceae	*Jablonskia congesta*	padozinho, padorina
Euphorbiaceae	*Mabea* cf. *caudata*	seringaí

FAMILY	SPECIES NAME	LOCAL NAMES
Euphorbiaceae	*Mabea nitida*	seringaí
Euphorbiaceae	*Mabea paniculata*	seringaí, abiorana
Euphorbiaceae	*Micrandra siphonioides*	seringarana
Euphorbiaceae	*Nealchornea* sp.	-
Euphorbiaceae	*Omphalea diandra*	-
Euphorbiaceae	*Phyllanthus biantherifer*	padozinho
Euphorbiaceae	*Phyllanthus corcovadensis*	quebra-pedra
Euphorbiaceae	*Phyllanthus fluitans*	-
Euphorbiaceae	*Phyllanthus urinaria*	-
Euphorbiaceae	*Piranhea trifoliata*	piranheira
Euphorbiaceae	*Ricinus* spp. *	pião-roxo, pião-branco
Euphorbiaceae	*Sapium hippomane*	murupita
Euphorbiaceae	*Tragia* sp.	turimã-branco
Fagaceae	*Ilex* sp.	catinga-de-porco
Flacourtiaceae	*Banara nitida*	pingo-d'água-da-curica, farinha-seca
Flacourtiaceae	*Casearia aculeata*	limorana, limoranarana, turimã-amarelo
Flacourtiaceae	*Casearia benthamii*	espinho-de-judeu
Flacourtiaceae	*Eichlerodendron* cf. *calophyllum*	espinho-de-judeu
Flacourtiaceae	*Homalium racemosum*	sardinheira, turimã-branco
Flacourtiaceae	*Homalium* sp.	turimã-branco
Flacourtiaceae	*Laetia corymbulosa*	turimã, turimã-vermelho
Flacourtiaceae	*Xylosma intermedium*	espinho-de-judeu
Gentianaceae	*Coutoubea ramosa*	tingui
Gentianaceae	*Iribachia alata* spp. *alata*	-
Gentianaceae	*Voyria* sp.	-
Guttiferae	*Calophyllum brasiliense*	jacareúba
Guttiferae	*Clusia* cf. *panapanari*	apuí
Guttiferae	*Clusia* cf. *platystigma*	apuí
Guttiferae	*Clusia criuvopoidia*	apuí-de-baladeira
Guttiferae	*Clusia* sp.	apuí-de-baladeira
Guttiferae	*Garcinia gardneriana*	-
Guttiferae	*Garcinia macrophylla*	bacuri-coroa
Guttiferae	*Rheedia acuminata*	bacuri-coroa
Guttiferae	*Rheedia brasiliensis*	bacuri
Guttiferae	*Rheedia macrophylla*	bacuri-liso
Guttiferae	*Tovomita brasiliensis*	paxiubarana
Guttiferae	*Tovomita cephalostigma*	paxiubinha, paxiubarana-folha-média
Guttiferae	*Tovomita* cf. *rostrata*	paxiubarana
Guttiferae	*Tovomita speciosa*	paxiubarana, paxiubarana-folha-grande
Guttiferae	*Tovomita triflora*	paxiubarana
Guttiferae	*Vismia* aff. *cayennensis*	lacre, lacre-da-folha-fina, lacre-branca
Guttiferae	*Vismia macrophylla*	lacre-da-folha-larga, lacre-folha-grande
Hippocrateaceae	*Cheiloclinium* sp.	cipó
Hippocrateaceae	*Hippocratea* sp. 1	cipó-crista-de-galo
Hippocrateaceae	*Hippocratea* sp. 2	cipó-preto
Hippocrateaceae	Não identificada	jararabucha
Hippocrateaceae	*Peritassa* cf. *laexigata*	cipó-ovo-de-guariba, jatumã
Hippocrateaceae	*Peritassa dulcis*	jatumã
Hippocrateaceae	*Salacia* aff. *megistophylla*	xixuaxa
Hippocrateaceae	*Salacia* cf. *impressifolia*	cipó-enrrugado, cipó-mucunã, cipó-rajado, cipó-preto, papo-de-mututi

FAMILY	SPECIES NAME	LOCAL NAMES
Hippocrateaceae	*Salacia* sp.	cipó-ovo-de-guariba, gogó-de-velho, xixuaxa
Icacinaceae	*Dendrobangia* sp.	-
Labiatae	*Leucas martinicensis**	mulata-catinga
Labiatae	*Mentha viridis**	hortelã
Labiatae	*Ocimum micranthum*	alfavaca
Lacistemataceae	*Lacistema* cf. *aggregatum*	caferanarana, acapuí, caferana
Lauraceae	*Aniba guianensis*	louro-abacate, louro-abacaterana
Lauraceae	*Aniba* sp.	louro-abacate, louro-amarelo
Lauraceae	*Endlicheria bracteata*	louro-babão
Lauraceae	*Licaria amara*	louro
Lauraceae	*Licaria armeniaca*	louro-chumbo-folha-miúda
Lauraceae	*Mezilaurus* sp.	itaúba
Lauraceae	*Não identificada*	louro-fogo
Lauraceae	*não identificada*	louro-jacaré
Lauraceae	*Nectandra amazonum*	louro-chumbo, lourinho, louro-branco
Lauraceae	*Nectandra* cf. *marmellensis*	louro-amarelo
Lauraceae	*Nectandra* sp.	louro-preto
Lauraceae	*Ocotea aplendens*	louro-chumbo
Lauraceae	*Ocotea barcellensis*	louro
Lauraceae	*Ocotea cernua*	louro-chumbo-folha-grande
Lauraceae	*Ocotea cymbarum*	louro-inamuí
Lauraceae	*Ocotea opifera* (ou *Aniba*)	louro-abacate
Lauraceae	*Ocotea* spp.	louro, louro-abacate, louro-amarelo, louro-bosta, louro-preto, lourinho
Lauraceae	*Ocotea wachenheimii*	louro-chumbo
Lauraceae	*Persea americana**	abacate
Lecythidaceae	*Bertholetia excelsa**	castanha-do-pará
Lecythidaceae	*Couroupita guianensis*	macacaricuia
Lecythidaceae	*Couroupita* sp.	macacaricuia
Lecythidaceae	*Eschweilera albiflora*	matá-matá
Lecythidaceae	*Eschweilera amazonica*	ripeira
Lecythidaceae	*Eschweilera parvifolia*	ripeira
Lecythidaceae	*Eschweilera* sp.	castanharana
Lecythidaceae	*Eschweilera tenuifolia*	matá-matá, matá-matá-folha-grande
Lecythidaceae	*Gustavia hexapetala*	carambolinha, cachimbo-fedorento, genipaporana, geniparana, genipapinho
Lecythidaceae	*Lecythis paraensis*	sapucaia
Lecythidaceae	*Lecythis pisonis*	castanha-sapucaia
Lentibulariaceae	*Utricularia foliosa*	-
Lentibulariaceae	*Utricularia* sp. 1	-
Lentibulariaceae	*Utricularia* sp. 2	-
Loganiaceae	*Strychnos asperula*	gogó-de-guariba
Loganiaceae	*Strychnos darienensis*	-
Loganiaceae	*Strychnos mattogrossensis*	gogó-de-guariba, cipó-cuia
Loganiaceae	*Strychnos nigricans*	-
Loganiaceae	*Strychnos rondeletoides*	-
Loganiaceae	*Strychnos* sp.	cipó-cuia, cipó-ferro
Lythraceae	*Cuphea melvilla*	-
Malpighiaceae	*Byrsonima* aff. *arthropoda*	-
Malpighiaceae	*Byrsonima amazonica*	muruxi
Malpighiaceae	*Byrsonima japurensis*	muruci, muruxi

FAMILY	SPECIES NAME	LOCAL NAMES
Malpighiaceae	*Byrsonima* sp.	muruci, muruci-da-restinga
Malpighiaceae	cf. *Hiraea fagigolia*	-
Malpighiaceae	*Mascagnia divaricata*	-
Malpighiaceae	*Stigmaphyllon* aff. *paraense*	-
Malpighiaceae	*Stigmaphyllon sinuatum*	-
Malvaceae	*Gossypium* aff. *barbadense*	algodão
Malvaceae	*Hibiscus bifurcatus*	-
Malvaceae	*Hibiscus rosa-sinensis**	pampola
Malvaceae	*Hibiscus sororis*	-
Malvaceae	*Malachra radiata*	-
Malvaceae	*Melochia mollis*	-
Melastomataceae	*Aciotis aequatorialis*	-
Melastomataceae	*Miconia calvascens*	-
Melastomataceae	*Miconia poeppigii*	-
Melastomataceae	*Mouriri acutifolia*	socoró
Melastomataceae	*Mouriri nigra*	socoró
Melastomataceae	*Mouriri* sp.	araçá, araçá-branco, araçá-de-macaco, macaco, saboarana
Melastomataceae	*Mouriri ulei*	socoró
Melastomataceae	*Tococa* ou *Maieta* spp.	-
Meliaceae	*Carapa guianensis*	andiroba
Meliaceae	*Cedrela* cf. *odorata*	cedro, cedrinho
Meliaceae	*Guarea subssessiliflora*	jitó
Meliaceae	*Trichilia lecointei*	bico-de-brasa
Meliaceae	*Trichilia micrantha*	bico-de-brasa-da-restinga, jitó
Meliaceae	*Trichilia solitudinis*	bico-de-brasa
Menispermaceae	*Cissampelos pareira*	-
Menispermaceae	*Cissampelos* sp.	-
Menispermaceae	*Curarea toxifera*	-
Menispermaceae	*Odontocarya tamoides*	-
Mimosaceae	*Acacia paniculata*	-
Mimosaceae	*Acacia polyphylla*	espinheiro
Mimosaceae	*Albizia corymbosa*	-
Mimosaceae	*Entada polyphylla*	cipó-escova, jipioca
Mimosaceae	*Entada* sp.	-
Mimosaceae	*Inga bourgoni*	ingá
Mimosaceae	*Inga* cf. *coriacea*	ingá
Mimosaceae	*Inga cinnamomea*	ingá-açu
Mimosaceae	*Inga distincha*	ingá, ingá-peluda
Mimosaceae	*Inga duckei*	-
Mimosaceae	*Inga dumosa*	ingá
Mimosaceae	*Inga marginata*	ingá
Mimosaceae	*Inga microcalyx*	ingá
Mimosaceae	*Inga myriantha*	ingá
Mimosaceae	*Inga paraensis*	-
Mimosaceae	*Inga punctata*	-
Mimosaceae	*Inga rubiginosa*	ingá
Mimosaceae	*Inga* sp. 1	ingá-de-morcego
Mimosaceae	*Inga* sp. 2	ingá-de-sapo
Mimosaceae	*Inga thibaudiana*	ingá-barata
Mimosaceae	*Inga vera*	-

FAMILY	SPECIES NAME	LOCAL NAMES
Mimosaceae	*Mimosa diplocarpa*	-
Mimosaceae	*Mimosa orthocarpa*	-
Mimosaceae	*Mimosa pigra*	-
Mimosaceae	*Neptunia plena* ou *oleracea*	-
Mimosaceae	*Neptunia* sp.	-
Mimosaceae	*Pithecellobium corymbosum*	paricarana
Mimosaceae	*Pithecellobium inaequale*	ingá-de-sapo
Mimosaceae	*Pithecellobium jupumba*	mari-mari bravo
Mimosaceae	*Pithecellobium multiflorum*	mari-mari bravo
Mimosaceae	*Pithecellobium* spp.	ingá-do-cão, ingá-de-cigana, mututi-da-folha-fina
Mimosoideae	*Inga edulis**	ingá-cipó
Moraceae	*Artocarpus altilis**	fruta-pão
Moraceae	*Artocarpus* sp.*	jaca
Moraceae	*Batocarpus amazonicus*	pau-pajé
Moraceae	*Brosimum lactescens*	manixi, manixi-preto, muirapiranga, muiratinga-rapé-do-índio
Moraceae	*Chlorophora tinctoria*	limorana
Moraceae	*Ficus amazonica*	apuí
Moraceae	*Ficus antihelminthica*	gaxinguba-lombrigueira
Moraceae	*Ficus* cf. *hebetifolia*	apuí
Moraceae	*Ficus* cf. *pertusa*	apuí
Moraceae	*Ficus guianensis*	apuí
Moraceae	*Ficus insipida*	gaxinguba
Moraceae	*Ficus maxima*	apuí, apuí-grande, gameleira, caxinguba, gaxinguba
Moraceae	*Ficus schumacheri*	apuí-folha-fina, apuí
Moraceae	*Ficus trigona*	apuí
Moraceae	*Maclura tinctoria*	-
Moraceae	*Maquira coriacea*	muiratinga, muiratinga-da-várzea, muiratinga-do-igapó, apuí
Moraceae	*Pourouma cecropeafolia**	purumã
Moraceae	*Pseudolmedia laevicarpa*	pamã, abiorana
Moraceae	*Pseudolmedia laevigata*	manixi-liso
Moraceae	*Sorocea duckei*	caimbé
Myristicaceae	*Iryanthera juruensis*	ucuubinha
Myristicaceae	*Iryanthera macrophylla*	ucuuba-folha-grande
Myristicaceae	*Iryanthera olacoides*	ucuúba
Myristicaceae	*Iryanthera* sp.	ucuubinha
Myristicaceae	*Virola cuspidata*	ucuúba
Myristicaceae	*Virola surinamensis*	virola, ucuúba
Myrtaceae	*Calycolpus goetheanus*	araçapeua
Myrtaceae	*Calyptranthes crebra*	gumorana
Myrtaceae	*Calyptranthes multiflora*	arati
Myrtaceae	*Calyptranthes* sp.	araçá
Myrtaceae	*Eugenia brachypoda*	araçá-amarelo
Myrtaceae	*Eugenia* cf. *omissa*	araçá-ferro, araçá, araçá-do-igapó
Myrtaceae	*Eugenia feijoi*	araçá-amarelo
Myrtaceae	*Eugenia inundata*	arati
Myrtaceae	*Eugenia jambo**	jambo
Myrtaceae	*Eugenia prosoneura*	araçapeua

FAMILY	SPECIES NAME	LOCAL NAMES
Myrtaceae	*Eugenia schomburgkii*	araçá-amarelo
Myrtaceae	*Eugenia* sp. 1	araçá-da-folha-grande, araçá-da-folha-fina, maria-preta
Myrtaceae	*Eugenia* sp. 2	araçá
Myrtaceae	*Eugenia* sp. 3	araçá-de-macaco
Myrtaceae	*Eugenia stipitata**	araçá-boi
Myrtaceae	*Marlierea* cf. *umbraticola*	araçá, araçá-preto
Myrtaceae	*Myrcia* cf. *rufipila*	araçá
Myrtaceae	*Myrcia coumete*	araçá
Myrtaceae	*Myrcia decorticans*	araçá-amarelo
Myrtaceae	*Myrcia fallax*	araçá-amarelo
Myrtaceae	*Myrcia* spp.	araçá, araçá-preto, gumorana, pingo-d'água, araçá-de-folha-fina
Myrtaceae	*Myrciaria dubia*	camu-camu
Myrtaceae	*Myrciaria floribunda*	araçapeua
Myrtaceae	*Myrciaria* sp.	araçapeua-folha-peluda
Myrtaceae	*Psidium* cf. *acutangulum*	araçá
Myrtaceae	*Psidium guajaba*	goiaba
Myrtaceae	*Psidium ovatifolium*	araçá
Myrtaceae	*Psidium* sp.	araçá, araçá-de-macaco
Nyctaginaceae	*Neea* cf. *aeruginosa*	violeta
Nyctaginaceae	*Neea* sp.	violeta, joão-mole
Nyctaginaceae	*Pisonia* sp.	sacaiti, violeta
Ochnaceae	*Blastomanthus* sp.	-
Ochnaceae	*Ouratea salicifolia*	mortinha, tinteiro
Olacaceae	*Cathedra acuminata*	bacuri-de-anta, marfim
Olacaceae	*Heisteria* cf. *densiflora*	-
Olacaceae	*Heisteria* sp.	-
Olacaceae	*Heisteria spruceana*	trec-trec, castanharana
Olacaceae	*Minquartia guianensis*	acapu-verdadeiro
Onagraceae	*Ludwigia affinis*	-
Onagraceae	*Ludwigia* cf. *rigida*	-
Onagraceae	*Ludwigia decurrens*	-
Onagraceae	*Ludwigia helminthorhiza*	-
Onagraceae	*Ludwigia leptocarpa*	-
Onagraceae	*Ludwigia natans*	-
Onagraceae	*Ludwigia* spp.	-
Oxalidaceae	*Averrhoa carambola**	carambola
Papilionaceae	*Acosmium nitens*	anaxi, buiussu
Papilionaceae	*Acosmium* sp.	itaubarana
Papilionaceae	*Aeschynomene ciliata*	-
Papilionaceae	*Aeschynomene rudis*	-
Papilionaceae	*Aeschynomene sensitiva* var. *amazonica*	-
Papilionaceae	*Aeschynomene* sp.	-
Papilionaceae	*Andira inermis*	cumarurana
Papilionaceae	*Bocoa alterna*	-
Papilionaceae	*Clitoria amazonum*	fava-de-boto, paliteira, paliteira-brava
Papilionaceae	*Clitoria falcata*	fava-de-boto, paliteira, paliteira-brava
Papilionaceae	*Clitoria* sp.	baju
Papilionaceae	*Cymbosema roseum*	-
Papilionaceae	*Dalbergia inundata*	rabo-de-macaco

FAMILY	SPECIES NAME	LOCAL NAMES
Papilionaceae	*Dalbergia riparia*	rabo-de-guariba, rabo-de-macaco, rabo-de-macaquinho
Papilionaceae	*Dalbergia* sp.	cipó-grosso
Papilionaceae	*Derris* spp.	buiussu, timbó, rabo-de-guariba
Papilionaceae	*Dioclea* aff. *virgata*	-
Papilionaceae	*Dioclea glabra*	-
Papilionaceae	*Erythrina fusca*	-
Papilionaceae	*Etaballia guianensis*	mututi-branco
Papilionaceae	*Etaballia* sp.	mututi-ferro, mututim
Papilionaceae	*Lecointea amazonica*	paracuúba
Papilionaceae	*Lonchocarpus sericeus*	-
Papilionaceae	*Machaerium altiscandens*	cipó, unha-de-gato, rabo de guariba
Papilionaceae	*Machaerium lunnatum*	cipó
Papilionaceae	*Machaerium* sp.	cipó, unha-de-gato
Papilionaceae	*Mucuna altissima*	cipó-bico-de-mutum
Papilionaceae	*Mucuna rostrata*	cipó-bico-de-mutum
Papilionaceae	*Ormosia macrocalyx*	tento, tento-vermelho
Papilionaceae	*Ormosia nobilis*	tento-preto
Papilionaceae	*Paramachaerium ormosioides*	mututi
Papilionaceae	*Platymiscium ulei*	macacaúba
Papilionaceae	*Poecilanthe* sp.	anaxi, pé-de-burro
Papilionaceae	*Pterocarpus amazonicus*	mututi-branco
Papilionaceae	*Pterocarpus amazonum*	tachi-branco
Papilionaceae	*Pterocarpus ulei*	tachi-branco
Papilionaceae	*Sesbania exasperata*	-
Papilionaceae	*Swartzia* spp.	guajará, mututi
Papilionaceae	*Vatairea guianensis*	bau-bau, bau-bauzinho, faveira
Papilionaceae	*Vatairea* sp.	baú-baú, baú-bauzinho
Papilionaceae	*Vigna jururuana*	-
Papilionaceae	*Vigna lasiocarpa*	-
Papilionaceae	*Vigna unguiculata*	-
Passifloraceae	*Passiflora coccinea*	-
Passifloraceae	*Passiflora filipes*	-
Passifloraceae	*Passiflora glandulosa*	maracujá
Phytolacaceae	*Petiveria alliaceae**	mucura-caá
Phytolacaceae	*Microtea debilis*	-
Phytolacaceae	*Seguieria* sp.	cipó
Phytolacaceae	*Trichostigma octandra*	-
Piperaceae	*Piper peltata*	pimenta
Piperaceae	*Piper* sp. 1	-
Piperaceae	*Piper* sp. 2	-
Polygalaceae	*Diclidanthera penduliflora*	-
Polygonaceae	*Coccoloba* cf. *densifrons*	tanará-branco, tucunaré
Polygonaceae	*Coccoloba ovata*	tachi-branco, tanará
Polygonaceae	*Coccoloba pichuna*	tachi-branco, tanará-vermelho, tanará
Polygonaceae	*Polygonum acuminatum*	-
Polygonaceae	*Ruprechtia asperula*	-
Polygonaceae	*Ruprechtia laugorana*	tachi-preto
Polygonaceae	*Ruprechtia tangarana*	tachi-preto
Polygonaceae	*Ruprechtia tenuifolia*	-
Polygonaceae	*Symmeria paniculata*	carauaçu, tanará, caraiperana

FAMILY	SPECIES NAME	LOCAL NAMES
Polygonaceae	*Symmeria* sp.	louro-branco
Polygonaceae	*Triplaris pyramidalis*	tachi-vermelho
Polygonaceae	*Triplaris surinamensis*	tachi
Proteaceae	*Roupala* sp.	catinga-de-porco
Quiinaceae	*Quiina paraensis*	caferana
Quiinaceae	*Quiina rhytidopus*	caferana-sangrenta
Rhammaceae	*Rapanea ferrugina**	azeitona
Rhammaceae	*Colubrina* aff. *retusa*	pingo-d'água-do-macaco-prego
Rhammaceae	*Gouania frangulaeifolia*	pingo-d'água-do-macaco-prego
Rhizophoraceaea	*Sterigmapetalum* sp.	-
Rubiaceae	*Alibertia latifolia*	goiabinha-do-igapó
Rubiaceae	*Alibertia* sp.	goiabinha-do-igapó
Rubiaceae	*Bothriospora corymbosa*	pimenta-de-macaco
Rubiaceae	*Calycophyllum spruceanum*	mulateiro
Rubiaceae	*Coussarea hydrangifolia*	-
Rubiaceae	*Coussarea* sp.	pau-fedorento
Rubiaceae	*Coutarea* sp.	limoranarana, carapanaubarana
Rubiaceae	*Diodia teres*	pau-fedorento
Rubiaceae	*Duroia duckei*	genipapinho, genipapo-do-igapó
Rubiaceae	*Duroia macrophylla*	puruí
Rubiaceae	*Faramea* sp.	pau-fedorento
Rubiaceae	*Genipa americana*	genipapo
Rubiaceae	*Guettarda aromatica*	-
Rubiaceae	*Guettarda pohliana*	unha-de-cigana
Rubiaceae	*Não identificada*	-
Rubiaceae	*Oldenlandia corymbosa*	-
Rubiaceae	*Oldenlandia lanceifolia*	-
Rubiaceae	*Palicourea* aff. *decipiens*	-
Rubiaceae	*Palicourea* cf. *guianensis*	-
Rubiaceae	*Palicourea crocea*	-
Rubiaceae	*Palicourea* sp.	-
Rubiaceae	*Posoqueria longiflora*	araçá
Rubiaceae	*Psycotria lupulina*	-
Rubiaceae	*Rudgea cornifolia*	-
Rubiaceae	*Sickingia tinctoria*	pau-brasil
Rubiaceae	*Sommera sabicoides*	-
Rubiaceae	*Sommera* sp.	-
Rubiaceae	*Spermacoce latifolia*	-
Rubiaceae	*Spermacoce ocymifolia*	-
Rubiaceae	*Tocoyena foetida*	-
Rubiaceae	*Uncaria guianensis*	-
Rutaceae	*Citrus aurantifolia**	lima
Rutaceae	*Citrus limonia**	limão-comum
Rutaceae	*Citrus nobilis**	tangerina
Rutaceae	*Citrus sinensis**	laranja
Rutaceae	*Fagara* sp.	açacurana
Rutaceae	*Ruta graveolens**	arruda
Rutaceae	*Zanthoxylum reidelianum*	tamanqueira
Rutaceae	*Zanthoxylum* sp.	açacurana
Sapindaceae	*Allophylus amazonicus*	pingo-d'água-verdadeiro, olho-de-peixe
Sapindaceae	*Allophylus scrobiculatus*	-

FAMILY	SPECIES NAME	LOCAL NAMES
Sapindaceae	*Cupania* sp.	-
Sapindaceae	*Matayba arborescens*	farinha-seca, tento-de-piranha
Sapindaceae	*Matayba macrostylis*	farinha-seca, frutinha
Sapindaceae	*Paulinia alata*	-
Sapindaceae	*Paulinia* sp.	-
Sapindaceae	*Talisia* sp.	guelra-de-tambaqui, pitomba
Sapotaceae	*Chlorolema* cf. *gonocarpa*	abiorana-branca
Sapotaceae	*Chrysophyllum auratum*	abiorana, abiorana-de-macaco
Sapotaceae	*Elaeoluma glabrescens*	caramuri
Sapotaceae	*Franchetella anibifolia*	abiorana
Sapotaceae	*Franchetella* sp.	abiorana
Sapotaceae	*Micropholis egensis*	chupeta-de-vaca, mamita-de-peixe-boi
Sapotaceae	*Neoxythece elegans*	guajará, chupeta-de-vaca, maparajuba-da-restinga, abiorana-branca, maparajuba-grande
Sapotaceae	*Neoxythece* sp.	maparajuba-grande
Sapotaceae	*Pouteria caimito*	abiorana, abio
Sapotaceae	*Pouteria glomerata*	abiorana
Sapotaceae	*Pouteria gomphiifolia*	jará, caramuri, guajararana, ajaraí, camuri
Sapotaceae	*Pouteria* sp.	abiorana-branca
Sapotaceae	*Sarcaulus brasiliensis*	-
Sapotaceae	*Urbanella excelsa*	abiorana-vermelha, maparajuba
Scrophulariaceae	*Bacopa connata*	-
Scrophulariaceae	*Bacopa depressa*	-
Scrophulariaceae	*Bacopa egense*	-
Scrophulariaceae	*Lindernia crustacea*	-
Scrophulariaceae	*Lindernia procumbens*	-
Scrophulariaceae	*Scoparia dulcis*	vassourinha
Simarubaceae	*Simaba cedron*	-
Simarubaceae	*Simaba guianensis*	cajurana
Simarubaceae	*Simaba multiflora*	cajurana
Solanaceae	*Physalis angulata*	-
Solanaceae	*Solanum paniculatum*	-
Solanaceae	*Solanum sessiliforme*	cubiu
Solanaceae	*Solanum sisymbriifolium*	-
Solanaceae	*Solanum* sp. 2	-
Solanaceae	*Solanum* sp. 1	-
Sterculiaceae	*Byttneria ancistrodonta*	-
Sterculiaceae	*Byttneria coriacea*	espinho-de-moura
Sterculiaceae	*Guazuma ulmifolia*	mutamba
Sterculiaceae	*Herrania mariae*	cacauí
Sterculiaceae	*Sterculia elata*	tacacazeiro
Sterculiaceae	*Theobroma bicolor**	cacaurana
Sterculiaceae	*Theobroma cacao*	cacau
Sterculiaceae	*Theobroma grandiflorum*	cupuaçu
Sterculiaceae	*Theobroma guianense*	-
Sterculiaceae	*Theobroma mariae*	cacau-jacaré
Sterculiaceae	*Theobroma* sp.	cacau-morcego
Styracaceae	*Styrax guianensis*	murucututu, pau-pagão
Theophrastaceae	*Clavija lancifolia*	-
Tiliaceae	*Apeiba asperana*	boieira, bolacheira
Tiliaceae	*Apeiba* cf. *burchelli*	boieira, bolacheira

FAMILY	SPECIES NAME	LOCAL NAMES
Tiliaceae	*Luehea cymulosa*	icé, icerana
Tiliaceae	*Luehea* sp.	-
Ulmaceae	*Celtis aculeata*	-
Umbrelliferae	*Eryngium ckmanii*	chicória
Urtigaceaea	*Urera baccifera*	urtiga
Verbenaceae	*Lippia alba*	cidreira
Verbenaceae	*Lippia betulifolia*	-
Verbenaceae	*Phyla betulaeifolia*	-
Verbenaceae	*Vitex cymosa*	apuí, tarumã
Violaceae	*Corynostylis* sp.	-
Violaceae	*Leonia glycicarpa*	catoré, catoré-branco
Viscaceae	*Phoradendron platycaulon*	-
Vitaceae	*Cissus erosa*	-
Vitaceae	*Cissus* sicyoides	-
Vitaceae	*Cissus* sp.	-
Vochysiaceae	*Erisma calcaratum*	caraipé, caraiperana
Monocotiledonae		
Cyperaceae	*Eleocharis plicarhachis*	-
Cyperaceae	*Fimbriostylis diphylla*	-
Cyperaceae	*Fimbristylis littoralis*	-
Cyperaceae	*Rhynchospora* sp.	-
Dioscoreaceae	*Dioscorea dodecaneura*	-
Dioscoreaceae	*Dioscorea* sp.*	cará
Marantaceae	*Calathea micans*	pariri
Marantaceae	*Calathea microcephala*	-
Marantaceae	*Calathea* sp.	cauaçu
Orchidaceae	*Ionopsis utricularoides*	-
Orchidaceae	*Sobralia violacea*	-
Poaceae	*Echinochloa polystachya*	canarana
Poaceae	*Eragrostis hypnoides*	-
Poaceae	*Eragrostis japonica*	-
Poaceae	*Eriochloa punctata*	-
Poaceae	*Gimbopogon sativum**	capim-santo
Poaceae	*Guadua angustifolia*	bambu
Poaceae	*Guadua ciliata*	bambu
Poaceae	*Gynerium sagittatum*	-
Poaceae	*Hymenachne amplexicaule*	canarana
Poaceae	*Leersia hexandra*	arrozrana, arroz-bravo
Poaceae	*Leptochloa scabra*	-
Poaceae	*Luziola spruceana*	-
Poaceae	*Oryza grandiglumis*	-
Poaceae	*Oryza rufipogon* ou *sativa*	arrozrana
Poaceae	*Panicum dichotomiflorum*	-
Poaceae	*Panicum pilosum*	-
Poaceae	*Panicum poligonatum*	-
Poaceae	*Pariana tenuis*	-
Poaceae	*Paspalum conjugatum*	-
Poaceae	*Paspalum fasciculatum*	-
Poaceae	*Paspalum melanospermum*	-

FAMILY	SPECIES NAME	LOCAL NAMES
Poaceae	*Paspalum orbiculatum*	-
Poaceae	*Paspalum repens*	-
Poaceae	*Sacharum* sp.*	cana-de-açúcar
Poaceae	*Schizachyrium condensatum*	-
Poaceae	*Setaria* sp.	-
Poaceae	*Steinchisma* aff. *decipiens*	-
Zingiberaceae	*Costus scaber*	japaná
Zingiberaceae	*Crocus sativus**	açafrão
Zingiberaceae	*Não identificada*	japaná
GYMNOSPERMAE		
Gnetaceae	*Gnetum leyboldi*	itauá, ituá
Pteridiacea	*Ceratopteris pteridioides*	-

* Introduced and/or domesticated species.

3- FAUNA SPECIES OF MAMIRAUÁ

GROUP	FAMILY	SPECIES NAME*	LOCAL NAMES
MAMMALIA			
Marsupialia	Didelphidae	*Didelphis marsupialis*	mucura
Marsupialia	Didelphidae	*Philander opossum*	mucura xixica
Xenarthra	Bradypodidae	*Bradypus variegatus*	preguiça-bentinho
Xenarthra	Megalonychidae	*Choloepus didactylus*	preguiça-real
Xenarthra	Myrmecophagidae	*Tamandua tetradactyla*	tamanduá-mirim, t.-de-colete
Primates	Callitrichidae	*Cebuella pygmaea*	leãozinho, sauim-leãozinho
Primates	Cebidae	*Saimiri sciureus*	macaco-de-cheiro
Primates	Cebidae	*Saimiri vanzolinii*	macaco-de-cheiro
Primates	Cebidae	*Cebus apella*	macaco-prego
Primates	Cebidae	*Pithecia* sp.	parauacu
Primates	Cebidae	*Cacajao calvus*	uacari, bicó
Primates	Cebidae	*Alouatta seniculus*	guariba
Primates	Cebidae	*Ateles paniscus*	coatá, macaco-preto
Carnivora	Procyonidae	*Nasua nasua*	coati
Carnivora	Procyonidae	*Potos flavus*	jupará
Carnivora	Mustelidae	*Lutra longicaudis*	lontra, cachorro-de-água
Carnivora	Mustelidae	*Pteronura brasiliensis*	ariranha
Carnivora	Felidae	*Felis wiedii*	maracajá-peludo
Carnivora	Felidae	*Felis concolor*	onça-vermelha, suçuarana
Carnivora	Felidae	*Panthera onca*	onça-pintada, onça-preta
Artiodactyla	Tayassuidae	*Tayassu pecari*	queixada, porco-do-mato
Cetacea	Iniidae	*Inia geoffrensis*	boto-vermelho, boto
Cetacea	Delphinidae	*Sotalia fluviatilis*	tucuxi
Sirenia	Trichechidae	*Trichechus inunguis*	peixe-boi
Rodentia/Sciuromorpha	Sciuridae	*Sciurus* cf. *spadiceus*	quatipuru
Rodentia/Caviomorpha	Erethizontidae	*Coendou* cf. *prehensilis*	cuandu, porco-espinho, ouriço
Rodentia/Caviomorpha	Hidrochaeridae	*Hydrochaeris hydrochaeris*	capivara
Rodentia/Myomorpha	Echimyidae	*Isothrix bistriata*	rato-janem
Rodentia/Myomorpha	Echimyidae	*Dactylomys dactylinus*	coró, rato-coró
Rodentia/Myomorpha	Echimyidae	*Echimys* sp.	rato-espinhoso
AVES			
	Acciptridae	*Leptodon cayenensis*	gavião
	Acciptridae	*Chondrohierax uncinatus*	gavião
	Acciptridae	*Elanoides forficatus*	gavião-tesoura
	Acciptridae	*Harpagus bidentatus*	gavião
	Acciptridae	*Rostrhamus sociabilis*	gavião-bico-de-gancho
	Acciptridae	*Rostrhamus hamatus*	gavião
	Acciptridae	*Ictinea plumbea*	gavião, tauató
	Acciptridae	*Geranospiza caerulescens*	gavião
	Acciptridae	*Accipiter superciliosus*	gavião
	Acciptridae	*Leucopternis schistacea*	gavião-de pernas-vermelhas
	Acciptridae	*Buteogallus urubitinga*	gavião-preto
	Acciptridae	*Busarellus nigricolis*	gavião-panema, gavião-balaio
	Acciptridae	*Buteo magnirostris*	inéia, gavião-pega-pinto, inajá
	Acciptridae	*Buteo brachyurus*	gavião

GROUP	FAMILY	SPECIES NAME*	LOCAL NAMES
	Acciptridae	*Buteo nitidus*	gavião
	Acciptridae	*Harpia harpya*	gavião-real
	Acciptridae	*Spizastur melanoleucus*	gavião
	Acciptridae	*Spizaetus ornatus*	gavião
	Acciptridae	*Spizaetus tyrannus*	gavião
	Alcedinidae	*Ceryle torquata*	ariramba-grande
	Alcedinidae	*Chloroceryle amazona*	ariramba-dos-médio
	Alcedinidae	*Chloroceryle americana*	ariramba-pequeno
	Alcedinidae	*Chloroceryle inda*	ariramba-de-igarapé
	Alcedinidae	*Chloroceryle aenea*	ariramba-miudinho
	Anatidae	*Dendrocygna autumalis*	marreca, marreco
	Anatidae	*Amazonetta brasiliensis*	marrequinha
	Anatidae	*Neochen jubata*	marrecão
	Anatidae	*Cairina moschata*	pato
	Anhimidae	*Anhima cornuta*	alencó, alencorne, anhuma
	Anhingidae	*Anhinga anhinga*	carará, muiá-tinga, biguatinga
	Apodidae	*Streptoprocne zonaris*	-
	Apodidae	*Cypseloides* cf. *senex*	-
	Apodidae	*Chaetura cinereiventris*	-
	Apodidae	*Chaetura spinicauda*	-
	Apodidae	*Chaetura brachyura*	-
	Apodidae	*Panyptila cayennensis*	-
	Aramidae	*Aramus guarauna*	carão
	Ardeidae	*Ardea cocoi*	maguari
	Ardeidae	*Egretta alba*	garça-branca
	Ardeidae	*Egretta thula*	garça-branca-pequena
	Ardeidae	*Egretta caerulea*	-
	Ardeidae	*Butorides striatus*	socozinho
	Ardeidae	*Bubulcus ibis*	garça-dos-bois
	Ardeidae	*Agamia agami*	socó-azul
	Ardeidae	*Pilherodius pileatus*	garça-morena, garça-real
	Ardeidae	*Nycticorax nycticorax*	-
	Ardeidae	*Cochearius cochlearius*	arapapá
	Ardeidae	*Tigrissoma lineatus*	socó-onça, socó-boi
	Ardeidae	*Ixobrychus exilis*	-
	Bucconidae	*Notharcus tectus*	joão-bobo
	Bucconidae	*Bucco macrodactylus*	joão-bobo
	Bucconidae	*Bucco tamatia*	joão-bobo
	Bucconidae	*Nonnula rubecula*	-
	Bucconidae	*Monasa nigrifrons*	bico-de-brasa
	Capitonidae	*Capito aurovirens*	uru
	Caprimulgidae	*Chordeiles rupestris*	bacurau-da-praia
	Caprimulgidae	*Chordeiles minor*	-
	Caprimulgidae	*Podager nacunda*	-
	Caprimulgidae	*Nyctiprogne leucopyga*	bacurau
	Caprimulgidae	*Nyctidromus albicollis*	bacurau
	Caprimulgidae	*Hydropsalis climacocerca*	bacurau
	Cathartidae	*Sarcoramphus papa*	urubu-rei
	Cathartidae	*Coragyps atratus*	urubu
	Cathartidae	*Cathartes aura*	urubu-cabeça-vermelha
	Cathartidae	*Cathartes burrovianus*	urubu-cabeça-amarela
	Cathartidae	*Cathartes melambrotos*	urubu-cabeça-amarela
	Charadriidae	*Vanellus cayanus*	maçarico

GROUP	FAMILY	SPECIES NAME*	LOCAL NAMES
	Charadriidae	*Pluvialis dominica*	maçarico
	Charadriidae	*Charadrius collaris*	-
	Ciconidae	*Mycteria americana*	jaburu
	Columbridae	*Columba cayennensis*	pomba
	Columbridae	*Columba subvinaceae*	pomba
	Columbridae	*Columbina passerina*	rolinha
	Columbridae	*Leptotila rufaxilla*	juriti
	Cracidae	*Mitu tuberosa*	mutum-fava, mutum-açu
	Cracidae	*Crax globulosa*	mutum-piuri
	Cracidae	*Pipile cumanensis*	cujubim, jacutinga
	Cucculidae	*Coccyzus cinereus*	-
	Cucculidae	*Coccyzus americanus*	-
	Cucculidae	*Coccyzus euleri*	-
	Cucculidae	*Coccyzus melacoryphus*	-
	Cucculidae	*Piaya minuta*	ticuã-pequeno
	Cucculidae	*Piaya cayana*	ticuã
	Cucculidae	*Crotophaga major*	coroca
	Cucculidae	*Crotophaga ani*	anu-preto
	Cucculidae	*Tapera naevia*	matin, matintin
	Eurypygidae	*Eurypyga helias*	pavãozinho, pavão
	Falconidae	*Daptrius ater*	cancão, grogotori
	Falconidae	*Daptrius americanus*	gavião
	Falconidae	*Milvago chimachima*	cacaraí, pinhé
	Falconidae	*Micrastur semitorquatus*	gavião
	Falconidae	*Herpetotheres cachinnans*	acauã
	Falconidae	*Falco rufigularis*	morcegueiro
	Falconidae	*Falco peregrinus*	gavião
	Galbulidae	*Galbacyrhynchus leucotis*	dorminhoco
	Galbulidae	*Galbula tombaceae*	beija-flor-grande
	Galbulidae	*Jacamerops aurea*	beija-flor-grande
	Heliornithidae	*Heliornis fulica*	patinha-do-igapó
	Jacanidae	*Jacana jacana*	piaçoca, jaçanã
	Laridae	*Larus* cf. *pipixcan*	gaivota
	Laridae	*Phaetusa simplex*	gaivota
	Laridae	*Sterna hirundo*	gaivotinha
	Laridae	*Sterna superciliaris*	gaivotinha
	Laridae	*Rhynchops niger*	talha-mar
	Nyctibiidae	*Nyctibius grandis*	-
	Nyctibiidae	*Nyctibius griseus*	mãe-da-lua
	Opisthocomidae	*Ophistocomus hoazin*	cigana
	Pandionidae	*Pandion haeliatus*	caripira
	Phalacrocoracidae	*Phalacrocorax brasilianus*	miuá, biguá, mergulhão
	Picidae	*Picumnus* cf. *pumilus*	pinica-pauzinho
	Picidae	*Melanerpes cruentatus*	pinica-pau
	Picidae	*Veniliornis passerinus*	pinica-pau
	Picidae	*Piculus chrysochorus*	pinica-pau
	Picidae	*Chrysoptilus punctigula*	pinica-pau
	Picidae	*Celeus gramnicus*	pinica-pau
	Picidae	*Celeus elegans*	pinica-pau
	Picidae	*Celeus flavus*	pinica-pau-amarelo
	Picidae	*Celeus torquatus*	pinica-pau
	Picidae	*Dryocopus lineatus*	pinica-pau-de-cabeça-vermelha
	Picidae	*Campephilus melanoleucus*	pinica-pau-de-cabeça-vermelha
	Psittacidae	*Ara manilata*	maracanã

GROUP	FAMILY	SPECIES NAME*	LOCAL NAMES
	Psittacidae	*Ara severa*	maracanã-grande
	Psittacidae	*Ara macao*	arara-vermelha
	Psittacidae	*Ara chloroptera*	arara-vermelha
	Psittacidae	*Ara ararauna*	arara-amarela
	Psittacidae	*Aratinga leucophthalmus*	maracanã
	Psittacidae	*Aratinga weddellii*	maracanã-cara-escura
	Psittacidae	*Aratinga pertinax*	periquito
	Psittacidae	*Pyrrhura melanura*	periquito
	Psittacidae	*Forpus xanthopterygius*	periquito-de-santo-antônio
	Psittacidae	*Brotogeris versicolurus*	periquito-asa-branca, p.-da-ilha
	Psittacidae	*Brotogeris sanctithomae*	periquito-brasileiro, p.-estrelinha
	Psittacidae	*Pionopsitta barrabandi*	periquito
	Psittacidae	*Graydidascalus brachyurus*	curica
	Psittacidae	*Pionus maximilani*	-
	Psittacidae	*Amazona autumalis*	papagaio
	Psittacidae	*Amazona festiva*	papa-cacau, papagaio
	Psittacidae	*Amazona amazonica*	curicão
	Psittacidae	*Amazona farinosa*	moleiro, papagaio
	Rallidae	*Aramides guarauna*	três-potes
	Rallidae	*Laterallus exilis*	-
	Rallidae	*Laterallus fasciatus*	-
	Rallidae	*Porphyrula martinica*	galo-d'água-azul
	Rallidae	*Porphyrula flavirostris*	galo-d'água-branco
	Ramphastidae	*Ramphastos toco*	tucano
	Ramphastidae	*Ramphastos culminatus*	tucano-rouco
	Ramphastidae	*Ramphastos tucanus*	tucano-assoviador
	Ramphastidae	*Pteroglossus castanotis*	araçari
	Ramphastidae	*Pteroglossus incriptus*	araçari
	Ramphastidae	*Pteroglossus azara*	araçari-de-peito-vermelho
	Scolopacidae	*Limnodromus griseus*	maçarico
	Scolopacidae	*Limosa haemastica*	maçarico
	Scolopacidae	*Tringa melaneuca*	maçarico
	Scolopacidae	*Tringa flavipes*	maçarico
	Scolopacidae	*Tringa solitaria*	maçarico
	Scolopacidae	*Actitis macularia*	maçarico
	Scolopacidae	*Calidris melanotos*	maçarico
	Scolopacidae	*Calidris fuscicolis*	maçarico
	Scolopacidae	*Micropalama himantopus*	maçarico
	Strigidae	*Otus choliba*	caburé
	Strigidae	*Otus watsonii*	-
	Strigidae	*Ciccaba huhula*	-
	Strigidae	*Lophostrix cristata*	-
	Strigidae	*Pulsatrix perspicillata*	corujão
	Strigidae	*Glaucidium brasilianum*	caburezinho
	Threskiornithidae	*Mesembrinibis cayennensis*	curubá, coró-coró
	Threskiornithidae	*Ajaia ajaja*	colhereira
	Tinamidae	*Crypturellus undulatus*	macucagua
	Trochilidae	*Glaucis hirsuta*	beija-flor
	Trochilidae	*Phaethornis superciliosus*	beija-flor
	Trochilidae	*Phaethornis hispidus*	beija-flor
	Trochilidae	*Phaethornis ruber*	beija-flor
	Trochilidae	*Florisuga mellivora*	beija-flor
	Trochilidae	*Campylopterus largipennis*	beija-flor
	Trochilidae	*Anthracothorax nigricollis*	beija-flor

GROUP	FAMILY	SPECIES NAME*	LOCAL NAMES
	Trochilidae	*Chlorestes notatus*	beija-flor
	Trochilidae	*Chlorostilbon mellisugus*	beija-flor
	Trochilidae	*Thalurania furcata*	beija-flor
	Trochilidae	*Leucippus chlorocercus*	beija-flor
	Trochilidae	*Amazilia fimbriata*	beija-flor
	Trochilidae	*Amazilia* cf. *lactea*	beija-flor
	Trochilidae	*Heliomaster longirostris*	beija-flor
	Trogonidae	*Trogon melanurus*	saracuã
	Trogonidae	*Trogon collaris*	saracuã
	Trogonidae	*Trogon curucui*	saracuã
	Trogonidae	*Trogon violaceus*	saracuã
Passeriformes	Cotingidae	*Porphyrolaema porphyrolaema*	-
Passeriformes	Cotingidae	*Cotinga maynana*	-
Passeriformes	Cotingidae	*Cotinga cayana*	-
Passeriformes	Cotingidae	*Iodopleura isabellae*	-
Passeriformes	Cotingidae	*Querula purpurata*	-
Passeriformes	Cotingidae	*Cephalopterus ornatus*	anambé-buzina
Passeriformes	Cotingidae	*Gymnoderus foetidus*	anambé-pombo
Passeriformes	Dendrocolaptidae	*Dendrocincla fuliginosa*	arapaçu
Passeriformes	Dendrocolaptidae	*Sittasomus griseicapillus*	arapaçu
Passeriformes	Dendrocolaptidae	*Glyphorhynchus spirurus*	arapaçu
Passeriformes	Dendrocolaptidae	*Dendrexetastes rufigula*	arapaçu
Passeriformes	Dendrocolaptidae	*Dendrocolaptes picumnus*	arapaçu
Passeriformes	Dendrocolaptidae	*Xiphocolaptes promeropirhynchus*	arapaçu
Passeriformes	Dendrocolaptidae	*Xiphorhynchus guttatus*	arapaçu
Passeriformes	Dendrocolaptidae	*Xiphorhynchus obsoletus*	arapaçu
Passeriformes	Dendrocolaptidae	*Xiphorhynchus picus*	arapaçu
Passeriformes	Dendrocolaptidae	*Xiphorhynchus necopinus*	arapaçu
Passeriformes	Dendrocolaptidae	*Nasica longirostris*	arapaçu-grande
Passeriformes	Dendrocolaptidae	*Campylorhamphus trochilirostris*	arapaçu-de-bico-torto
Passeriformes	Furnariidae	*Furnarius minor*	joão de-barro
Passeriformes	Furnariidae	*Furnarius leucopus*	joão-de-barro
Passeriformes	Furnariidae	*Synallaxis albigularis*	-
Passeriformes	Furnariidae	*Synallaxis gujanensis*	-
Passeriformes	Furnariidae	*Synallaris propinqua*	-
Passeriformes	Furnariidae	*Certhiaxis cinnamomea*	-
Passeriformes	Furnariidae	*Certhiaxis mustelina*	-
Passeriformes	Furnariidae	*Cranioleuca vulpina*	-
Passeriformes	Furnariidae	*Cranioleuca vulpecula*	-
Passeriformes	Furnariidae	*Metopothrix aurantiacus*	-
Passeriformes	Furnariidae	*Philydor pyrrhodes*	-
Passeriformes	Hirundinidae	*Tachycineta albiventer*	andorinha
Passeriformes	Hirundinidae	*Phaeoprogne tapera*	andorinha
Passeriformes	Hirundinidae	*Progne subis*	andorinha
Passeriformes	Hirundinidae	*Progne chalybea*	andorinha
Passeriformes	Hirundinidae	*Notiochelidon cyanoleuca*	andorinha
Passeriformes	Hirundinidae	*Stelgidopteryx ruficollis*	andorinha
Passeriformes	Hirundinidae	*Riparia riparia*	andorinha
Passeriformes	Hirundinidae	*Hirundo rustica*	andorinha
Passeriformes	Icterini	*Molothrus bonariensis*	-
Passeriformes	Icterini	*Scaphidura oryzivora*	araúna
Passeriformes	Icterini	*Psarocolius decumamus*	japó-preto
Passeriformes	Icterini	*Psarocolius viridis*	japó-preto
Passeriformes	Icterini	*Psarocolius angustifrons*	japó

GROUP	FAMILY	SPECIES NAME*	LOCAL NAMES
Passeriformes	Icterini	*Cacicus cela*	japim
Passeriformes	Icterini	*Cacicus solitarius*	-
Passeriformes	Icterini	*Lampropsar tanagrinus*	-
Passeriformes	Icterini	*Agelaius icterocephalus*	tangará-cabeça-amarela
Passeriformes	Icterini	*Gymnomystax mexicanus*	-
Passeriformes	Icterini	*Icterus jamacaii*	rouxinol
Passeriformes	Icterini	*Leistes militaris*	-
Passeriformes	Parulini	*Dendroica petechia*	-
Passeriformes	Parulini	*Dendroica striata*	-
Passeriformes	Parulini	*Geothlypis aequinoctialis*	-
Passeriformes	Piprinae	*Schiffornis major*	-
Passeriformes	Piprinae	*Tyranneutes stolzmanii*	-
Passeriformes	Piprinae	*Pipra filicauda*	-
Passeriformes	Polioptilinae	*Polioptila plumbea*	-
Passeriformes	Thamnophilidae	*Taraba major*	maracá-de-onça
Passeriformes	Thamnophilidae	*Sakesphorus canadensis*	mururé-de-crista
Passeriformes	Thamnophilidae	*Thamnophilus doliatus*	mururé-barrado, mururé-pedrês
Passeriformes	Thamnophilidae	*Thamnophilus cryptoleucus*	mururé-de-asa-pintada
Passeriformes	Thamnophilidae	*Thamnophilus schistaceus*	-
Passeriformes	Thamnophilidae	*Thamnomanes caesius*	-
Passeriformes	Thamnophilidae	*Myrmotherula (obscura)* sp. n.	-
Passeriformes	Thamnophilidae	*Myrmotherula surinamensis*	-
Passeriformes	Thamnophilidae	*Myrmotherula menetriesii*	-
Passeriformes	Thamnophilidae	*Myrmotherula assimilis*	maria-preta
Passeriformes	Thamnophilidae	*Hypocnemis cantator*	-
Passeriformes	Thamnophilidae	*Cercomacra cinerascens*	-
Passeriformes	Thamnophilidae	*Cercomacra nigrescens*	-
Passeriformes	Thamnophilidae	*Myrmochanes hemileucus*	-
Passeriformes	Thamnophilidae	*Sclateria naevia*	-
Passeriformes	Thamnophilidae	*Myrmoborus leucophrys*	-
Passeriformes	Thamnophilidae	*Myrmoborus lugubris*	-
Passeriformes	Thamnophilidae	*Myrmeciza hyperythra*	-
Passeriformes	Thamnophilidae	*Myrmeciza melanoceps*	-
Passeriformes	Thamnophilidae	*Hypocnemoides melanopogon*	-
Passeriformes	Thamnophilidae	*Phlegopsis nigromaculata*	-
Passeriformes	Thraupini/emberezini	*Conirostrum bicolor*	-
Passeriformes	Thraupini/emberezini	*Dacnis flaviventer*	-
Passeriformes	Thraupini/emberezini	*Tersina viridis*	-
Passeriformes	Thraupini/emberezini	*Euphonia chlorotica*	matinzinho
Passeriformes	Thraupini/emberezini	*Euphonia laniirostris*	matinzinho
Passeriformes	Thraupini/emberezini	*Euphonia chrysopasta*	-
Passeriformes	Thraupini/emberezini	*Tangara chilensis*	-
Passeriformes	Thraupini/emberezini	*Tangara xanhogastra*	-
Passeriformes	Thraupini/emberezini	*Tangara mexicana*	-
Passeriformes	Thraupini/emberezini	*Thraupis epicospus*	sanhaçu
Passeriformes	Thraupini/emberezini	*Thraupis palmarum*	-
Passeriformes	Thraupini/emberezini	*Ramphocelus carbo*	pipira
Passeriformes	Thraupini/emberezini	*Ramphocelus nigrogularis*	pipira-vermelha
Passeriformes	Thraupini/emberezini	*Trichothraupis penicillata*	-
Passeriformes	Thraupini/emberezini	*Nemosia pileata*	cabeça-preta
Passeriformes	Thraupini/emberezini	*Thlypopsis sordida*	-
Passeriformes	Thraupini/emberezini	*Schistochlamys melanopsis*	-
Passeriformes	Thraupini/emberezini	*Saltator maximus*	-
Passeriformes	Thraupini/emberezini	*Salator coerulescens*	pipirão

GROUP	FAMILY	SPECIES NAME*	LOCAL NAMES
Passeriformes	Thraupini/emberezini	*Paroaria gularis*	tangará
Passeriformes	Thraupini/emberezini	*Volatinia jacarina*	pretinho-pulador
Passeriformes	Thraupini/emberezini	*Sporophila americana*	-
Passeriformes	Thraupini/emberezini	*Sporophila bouvronides*	-
Passeriformes	Thraupini/emberezini	*Sporophila lineola*	-
Passeriformes	Thraupini/emberezini	*Sporophila caerulescens*	-
Passeriformes	Thraupini/emberezini	*Sporophila castaneiventris*	peito-vermelhinho
Passeriformes	Thraupini/emberezini	*Oryzoborus angolensis*	-
Passeriformes	Thraupini/emberezini	*Sicalis columbina*	amarelinho-do-capim
Passeriformes	Thraupini/emberezini	*Amnodramus aurifrons*	-
Passeriformes	Troglodytidae	*Donacobius atricapillus*	-
Passeriformes	Troglodytidae	*Campylorhynchus turdinis*	garrancheiro, catalão
Passeriformes	Troglodytidae	*Thryothorus coraya*	-
Passeriformes	Troglodytidae	*Thryothorus leucotis*	catalãozinho
Passeriformes	Troglodytidae	*Troglodytes aedon*	-
Passeriformes	Turdidae	*Turdus ignobilis*	-
Passeriformes	Turdidae	*Turdus Lawrencii*	-
Passeriformes	Turdidae	*Turdus hauxwelli*	sabiá
Passeriformes	Tyranninae	*Zimmerius gracilipes*	-
Passeriformes	Tyranninae	*Camptostoma obsletum*	-
Passeriformes	Tyranninae	*Phaeomyias murina*	-
Passeriformes	Tyranninae	*Tyrannulus elatus*	-
Passeriformes	Tyranninae	*Myiopagis gaimardii*	-
Passeriformes	Tyranninae	*Myiopagis flavivertex*	-
Passeriformes	Tyranninae	*Elaenia spectabilis*	-
Passeriformes	Tyranninae	*Elaenia pelzelni*	-
Passeriformes	Tyranninae	*Ochthoeca littoralis*	-
Passeriformes	Tyranninae	*Serpophaga hypoleuca*	-
Passeriformes	Tyranninae	*Stigmatura napensis*	-
Passeriformes	Tyranninae	*Capsiemps flaveola*	-
Passeriformes	Tyranninae	*Hemitriccus iohannis*	-
Passeriformes	Tyranninae	*Todirostrum maculatum*	tiri, tibiriçá
Passeriformes	Tyranninae	*Todirostrum latirostre*	-
Passeriformes	Tyranninae	*Tolmomyias sulphurescens*	-
Passeriformes	Tyranninae	*Tolmomyias poliocephalus*	-
Passeriformes	Tyranninae	*Tolmomyias flaviventris*	-
Passeriformes	Tyranninae	*Lathrotriccus euleri*	-
Passeriformes	Tyranninae	*Cnemotriccus fuscatus*	-
Passeriformes	Tyranninae	*Pyrocephalus rubinatus*	-
Passeriformes	Tyranninae	*Muscisaxicola fluviatilis*	-
Passeriformes	Tyranninae	*Knipolegus orenocensis*	-
Passeriformes	Tyranninae	*Arundinicola leucocephala*	cabecinha-branca
Passeriformes	Tyranninae	*Attila bolivianus*	-
Passeriformes	Tyranninae	*Rhytipterna simplex*	-
Passeriformes	Tyranninae	*Myiarchus ferox*	-
Passeriformes	Tyranninae	*Ramphotrigon ruficauda*	-
Passeriformes	Tyranninae	*Ramphotrigon megacephala*	-
Passeriformes	Tyranninae	*Pitangus sulphuratus*	bem-te-vi
Passeriformes	Tyranninae	*Philohydor lictor*	bem-te-vi
Passeriformes	Tyranninae	*Megarrhynchus pitangua*	bem-te-vi
Passeriformes	Tyranninae	*Myiozetetes similis*	bem-te-vi
Passeriformes	Tyranninae	*Myiozetetes granadensis*	-
Passeriformes	Tyranninae	*Conopias trivirgata*	bem-te-vi
Passeriformes	Tyranninae	*Myiodynastes maculatus*	bem-te-vi-riscado

GROUP	FAMILY	SPECIES NAME*	LOCAL NAMES
Passeriformes	Tyranninae	*Legatus leucophaius*	bem-te-vi
Passeriformes	Tyranninae	*Empidonomus varius*	-
Passeriformes	Tyranninae	*Griseotyrannus aurantiotrocristatus*	-
Passeriformes	Tyranninae	*Tyrannopsis sulphurea*	-
Passeriformes	Tyranninae	*Tyrannus melancholicus*	siriri
Passeriformes	Tyranninae	*Tyrannus savana*	tesoura
Passeriformes	Tyranninae	*Tyrannus albogularis*	siriri
Passeriformes	Tyranninae	*Pachyramphus rufus*	-
Passeriformes	Tyranninae	*Pachyramphus castaneus*	-
Passeriformes	Tyranninae	*Pachyramphus polychopterus*	-
Passeriformes	Tyranninae	*Pachyramphus minor*	-
Passeriformes	Tyranninae	*Tityra semifasciata*	urubitinga
Passeriformes	Tyranninae	*Tityra cayana*	-
Passeriformes	Virenidae	*Cyclarhis gujanensis*	-
Passeriformes	Vireonidae	*Vireo olivaceus*	-
Passeriformes	Vireonidae	*Hylophilus thoracicus*	-
REPTILIA			
Squamata	Iguanidae	*Iguana iguana*	iguana ou camaleão
Squamata	Polychrotidae	*Anolis fuscoauratus*	papa-vento
Squamata	Polychrotidae	*Anolis ortonii*	papa-vento
Squamata	Tropiduridae	*Uracentron azureum*	-
Squamata	Tropiduridae	*Uranoscodon superciliosus*	tamacuaré
Squamata	Gekkonidae	*Gonatodes humeralis*	-
Squamata	Gekkonidae	*Hemidactylus mabouia*	osga-comum, lagartixa
Squamata	Gekkonidae	*Lepidoblepharis heyerorum*	-
Squamata	Gymnophthalmidae	*Prionodactylus argulus*	-
Squamata	Teiidae	*Ameiva ameiva*	calango-verde
Squamata	Teiidae	*Kentropyx altamazonica*	calango
Squamata	Teiidae	*Crocodilurus lacertinus*	jacarerana
Squamata	Teiidae	*Dracaena guianensis*	jacuruxi, cabeça-encarnada
Squamata	Teiidae	*Tupinambis teguixin*	jacuraru
Squamata	Boidae	*Corallus enydris*	cobra-de-veado, suaçobóia
Squamata	Boidae	*Eunectes murinus*	sucuri
Squamata	Colubridae	*Atractus* sp.	cobra-falsa-coral
Squamata	Colubridae	*Chironius fuscus*	sacaibóia, cobra-cipó
Squamata	Colubridae	*Dipsas catesbyi*	dormideira, cobra-cipó
Squamata	Colubridae	*Helicops leopardinus*	cobra-d'água, jararaca-d'água
Squamata	Colubridae	*Hydrodynastes bicinctus*	coral-d'água, cobra-d'água
Squamata	Colubridae	*Hydrops triangularis*	cobra-d'água, falsa-coral
Squamata	Colubridae	*Oxybelis fulgidus*	cobra-cipó, cobra-verde
Squamata	Colubridae	*Siphlophis cervinus*	dormideira, cobra-cipó
Squamata	Colubridae	*Spilotes pullatus*	cainana, papa-ovo
Squamata	Colubridae	*Thamnodynastes* sp.	cobra-do-mato
Crocodilia	Alligatoridae	*Caiman crocodilus*	jacaré-tinga
Crocodilia	Alligatoridae	*Melanosuchus niger*	jacaré-açu
Crocodilia	Alligatoridae	*Paleosuchus trigonatus*	jacaré-coroa
Chelonia	Testudinidae	*Geochelone denticulata*	jabuti-amarelo
Chelonia	Chelidae	*Chelus fimbriatus*	matamatá
Chelonia	Pelomedusidae	*Podocnemis expansa*	tartaruga
Chelonia	Pelomedusidae	*Podocnemis sextuberculata*	iaçá, pitiú
Chelonia	Pelomedusidae	*Podocnemis unifilis*	tracajá, zé-prego

GROUP	FAMILY	SPECIES NAME*	LOCAL NAMES
AMPHIBIA			
Anura	Bufonidae	*Bufo marinus*	sapo-cururu
Anura	Bufonidae	*Bufo* gr. *"typhonius"*	sapo-folha
Anura	Dendrobatidae	*Epipedobates hahneli*	-
Anura	Hylidae	*Hyla fasciata*	-
Anura	Hylidae	*Hyla granosa*	-
Anura	Hylidae	*Hyla haraldschulzi*	-
Anura	Hylidae	*Hyla lanciformis*	-
Anura	Hylidae	*Hyla leucophyllata*	-
Anura	Hylidae	*Hyla punctata*	-
Anura	Hylidae	*Hyla raniceps*	-
Anura	Hylidae	*Hyla riveroi*	-
Anura	Hylidae	*Hyla rossalleni*	-
Anura	Hylidae	*Hyla wavrini*	-
Anura	Hylidae	*Hyla* sp. 1	-
Anura	Hylidae	*Hyla* sp. 2	-
Anura	Hylidae	*Osteocephalus leprieurii*	-
Anura	Hylidae	*Osteocephalus taurinus*	-
Anura	Hylidae	*Phrynohyas resinifictrix*	-
Anura	Hylidae	*Phrynohyas venulosa*	-
Anura	Hylidae	*Phyllomedusa tomopterna*	-
Anura	Hylidae	*Scinax signata*	-
Anura	Hylidae	*Scinax* sp.	-
Anura	Hylidae	*Sphaenorhynchus carneus*	-
Anura	Hylidae	*Sphaenorhynchus dorisae*	-
Anura	Hylidae	*Sphaenorhynchus lacteus*	-
Anura	Leptodactylidae	*Adenomera andreae*	-
Anura	Leptodactylidae	*Hydrolaetare schmidti*	-
Anura	Leptodactylidae	*Leptodactylus riveroi*	-
Anura	Leptodactylidae	*Leptodactylus* gr. *wagneri* sp. 1	-
Anura	Leptodactylidae	*Leptodactylus* gr. *wagneri* sp. 2	-
Anura	Pipidae	*Pipa pipa*	-
Anura	Pseudidae	*Lysapsus limellus*	-
Gymnophiona	Typhlonectidae	*Typhlonectes* sp. 1	-
Gymnophiona	Typhlonectidae	*Typhlonectes* sp. 2	-
PISCES			
Elasmobranchiomorphi	Carcharinidae	*Carcharinus leucas*	tubarão
Elasmobranchiomorphi	Potamotrygonidae	*Potamotrygon motoro*	arraia
Elasmobranchiomorphi	Potamotrygonidae	*Potamotrygon constellata*	arraia
Elasmobranchiomorphi	Potamotrygonidae	*Potamotrygon hystrix*	arraia
Teleostomi-Dipnoi	Lepidosirenidae	*Lepidosiren paradoxa*	pirambóia
Teleostomi-Actinopter.	Lepidosirenidae		
Clupeiformes	Clupeidae	*Pellona castelnaeana*	sardinhão
Clupeiformes	Clupeidae	*Pellona flavipinnis*	sardinhão, peixe-ouro
Clupeiformes	Engraulidae	*Lycengraulis batesii*	manjuba
Clupeiformes	Engraulidae	Engraulidae sp. indet. 1	manjuba
Clupeiformes	Engraulidae	Engraulidae sp. indet. 2	manjuba
Clupeiformes	Engraulidae	Engraulidae sp. indet. 3	manjuba
Osteoglossiformes	Osteoglossidae	*Arapaima gigas*	pirarucu
Osteoglossiformes	Osteoglossidae	*Osteoglossum bicirrhosum*	aruanã, açulamba
Cypriniformes-Characo.	Erythrinidae	*Erythrinus erythrinus*	jeju, aracapuri

GROUP	FAMILY	SPECIES NAME*	LOCAL NAMES
Cypriniformes-Characo.	Erythrinidae	*Hoplias malabaricus*	traíra
Cypriniformes-Characo.	Erythrinidae	*Hoploerythrinus unitaeniatus*	jeju
Cypriniformes-Characo.	Ctenoluciidae	*Boulengerella maculata*	peixe-agulhão
Cypriniformes-Characo.	Crenuchidae	*Crenuchus spilurus*	-
Cypriniformes-Characo.	Characidiidae	*Characidium (fasciatum)* sp. 1	-
Cypriniformes-Characo.	Characidiidae	*Characidium (fasciatum)* sp. 2	-
Cypriniformes-Characo.	Characidiidae	*Characidium* sp. 3	-
Cypriniformes-Characo.	Characidiidae	*Elachocharax pulcher*	-
Cypriniformes-Characo.	Anostomidae	*Abramites hypselonotus*	aracu
Cypriniformes-Characo.	Anostomidae	*Anostomoides laticeps*	aracu
Cypriniformes-Characo.	Anostomidae	*Laemolyta varia*	aracu
Cypriniformes-Characo.	Anostomidae	*Leporinus agassizi*	aracu
Cypriniformes-Characo.	Anostomidae	*Leporinus cylindriformis*	aracu
Cypriniformes-Characo.	Anostomidae	*Leporinus fasciatus*	aracu-flamengo
Cypriniformes-Characo.	Anostomidae	*Leporinus frederici*	aracu-piau, cabeça-gorda
Cypriniformes-Characo.	Anostomidae	*Leporinus trifasciatus*	aracu
Cypriniformes-Characo.	Anostomidae	*Pseudanos gracilis*	aracu
Cypriniformes-Characo.	Anostomidae	*Pseudanos trimaculatus*	aracu
Cypriniformes-Characo.	Anostomidae	*Rhytiodus microlepis*	aracu-de-boto
Cypriniformes-Characo.	Anostomidae	*Rhytiodus argenteofuscus*	aracu
Cypriniformes-Characo.	Anostomidae	*Rhytiodus* sp. 1	aracu-banana
Cypriniformes-Characo.	Anostomidae	*Schizodon fasciatum*	aracu-comum
Cypriniformes-Characo.	Hemiodontidae	*Anodus elongatus*	charuto
Cypriniformes-Characo.	Hemiodontidae	*Anodus melanopogon*	cubiu
Cypriniformes-Characo.	Hemiodontidae	*Hemiodopsis immaculatus*	orana-branca
Cypriniformes-Characo.	Hemiodontidae	*Hemiodopsis microlepis*	orana-flecheira
Cypriniformes-Characo.	Hemiodontidae	*Hemiodopsis gracilis*	orana
Cypriniformes-Characo.	Hemiodontidae	*Hemiodopsis goeldii*	orana
Cypriniformes-Characo.	Hemiodontidae	*Hemiodus unimaculatus*	orana
Cypriniformes-Characo.	Lebiasinidae	*Pyrrhulina* sp. 1	-
Cypriniformes-Characo.	Lebiasinidae	*Pyrrhulina* sp. 2	-
Cypriniformes-Characo.	Lebiasinidae	*Copella* cf. *arnoldi*	-
Cypriniformes-Characo.	Lebiasinidae	*Copella* gr. *nattereri*	-
Cypriniformes-Characo.	Lebiasinidae	*Nannobrycon eques*	-
Cypriniformes-Characo.	Lebiasinidae	*Nannobrycon unifasciatus*	-
Cypriniformes-Characo.	Lebiasinidae	*Nannostomus bifasciatus*	-
Cypriniformes-Characo.	Lebiasinidae	*Nannostomus harrisoni*	-
Cypriniformes-Characo.	Lebiasinidae	*Nannostomus trifasciatus*	-
Cypriniformes-Characo.	Lebiasinidae	*Nannostomus. marginatus*	-
Cypriniformes-Characo.	Chilodidae	*Chilodus punctatus*	-
Cypriniformes-Characo.	Chilodidae	*Chilodus* sp. 1	-
Cypriniformes-Characo.	Chilodidae	*Caenotropus labyrinthicus*	-
Cypriniformes-Characo.	Curimatidae	*Curimata* sp. 1	branquinha
Cypriniformes-Characo.	Curimatidae	*Curimata* sp. 2	branquinha
Cypriniformes-Characo.	Curimatidae	*Curimata vittata*	branquinha
Cypriniformes-Characo.	Curimatidae	*Curimatella alburna*	branquinha
Cypriniformes-Characo.	Curimatidae	*Curimatopsis* cf. *macrolepis*	branquinha
Cypriniformes-Characo.	Curimatidae	*Potamorhina latior*	branquinha-peito-de-aço
Cypriniformes-Characo.	Curimatidae	*Potamorhina altamazonica*	branquinha-comum
Cypriniformes-Characo.	Curimatidae	*Potamorhina pristigaster*	branquinha-cabeça-lisa
Cypriniformes-Characo.	Curimatidae	*Psectrogaster rutiloides*	cascudinha
Cypriniformes-Characo.	Curimatidae	*Psectrogaster amazonica*	cascudinha
Cypriniformes-Characo.	Prochilodontidae	*Prochilodus nigricans*	curimatá
Cypriniformes-Characo.	Prochilodontidae	*Semaprochilodus taeniurus*	jaraqui-escama-fina

GROUP	FAMILY	SPECIES NAME*	LOCAL NAMES
Cypriniformes-Characo.	Prochilodontidae	*Semaprochilodus theraponura*	jaraqui-escama-grossa
Cypriniformes-Characo.	Gasteropelecidae	*Carnegiella strigata*	sardinha-papuda
Cypriniformes-Characo.	Gasteropelecidae	*Gasteropelecus sternicla*	sardinha-papuda
Cypriniformes-Characo.	Serrasalmidae	*Colossoma macropomum*	tambaqui
Cypriniformes-Characo.	Serrasalmidae	*Metynnis* cf. *maculatus*	pacu-embaúba
Cypriniformes-Characo.	Serrasalmidae	*Myleus rubripinnis*	pacu-galo, pacutinga
Cypriniformes-Characo.	Serrasalmidae	*Myleus schomburgki*	pacu-jumento
Cypriniformes-Characo.	Serrasalmidae	*Myleus torquatus*	pacu-guariba
Cypriniformes-Characo.	Serrasalmidae	*Mylossoma duriventre*	pacu comum
Cypriniformes-Characo.	Serrasalmidae	*Mylossoma aureum*	pacu-manteiga
Cypriniformes-Characo.	Serrasalmidae	*Piaractus brachypomus*	pirapitinga
Cypriniformes-Characo.	Serrasalmidae	*Pygocentrus nattereri*	piranha-caju
Cypriniformes-Characo.	Serrasalmidae	*Serrasalmus elongatus*	piranha-mucura-branca
Cypriniformes-Characo.	Serrasalmidae	*Serrasalmus rhombeus*	piranha-preta
Cypriniformes-Characo.	Serrasalmidae	*Serrasalmus serrulatus*	piranha-pacu
Cypriniformes-Characo.	Serrasalmidae	*Serrasalmus* cf. *spilopleura*	piranha-branca
Cypriniformes-Characo.	Serrasalmidae	*Serrasalmus* sp. 2	piranha-amarela
Cypriniformes-Characo.	Serrasalmidae	*Serrasalmus* sp. 3	piranha-nazaré
Cypriniformes-Characo.	Serrasalmidae	*Serrasalmus* sp. 4	piranha-caju-roxo
Cypriniformes-Characo.	Serrasalmidae	*Serrasalmus* sp. 5	piranha-xidauá
Cypriniformes-Characo.	Serrasalmidae	*Serrasalmus* sp. 6	piranha-mucura-vermelha
Cypriniformes-Characo.	Characidae	*Agoniates anchovia*	-
Cypriniformes-Characo.	Characidae	*Acestrorhynchus falcatus*	peixe-agulhão
Cypriniformes-Characo.	Characidae	*Acestrorhynchus falcirostris*	peixe-agulhão
Cypriniformes-Characo.	Characidae	*Acestrorhynchus microlepis*	peixe-agulhão
Cypriniformes-Characo.	Characidae	*Aphyocharax alburnus*	-
Cypriniformes-Characo.	Characidae	*Asiphonichthys* cf. *condei*	-
Cypriniformes-Characo.	Characidae	*Astyanax bimaculatus*	matupiri
Cypriniformes-Characo.	Characidae	*Brycon melanopterus*	jatuarana, gogota
Cypriniformes-Characo.	Characidae	*Brycon* sp. 1	matrinchã
Cypriniformes-Characo.	Characidae	*Chalceus erythrurus*	arari-amarelo
Cypriniformes-Characo.	Characidae	*Chalceus macrolepidotus*	arari-vermelho
Cypriniformes-Characo.	Characidae	*Charax gibbosus*	-
Cypriniformes-Characo.	Characidae	*Ctenobrycon spilurus*	piaba
Cypriniformes-Characo.	Characidae	*Cynodon gibbus*	peixe-cachorro
Cypriniformes-Characo.	Characidae	*Hemigrammus ocellifer*	piaba
Cypriniformes-Characo.	Characidae	*Hemigrammus* gr. *ocellifer* sp. 1	piaba
Cypriniformes-Characo.	Characidae	*Hemigrammus* cf. *levis*	piaba
Cypriniformes-Characo.	Characidae	*Hemigrammus* cf. *pulcher*	piaba
Cypriniformes-Characo.	Characidae	*Hemigrammus* aff. *schmardae*	piaba
Cypriniformes-Characo.	Characidae	*Hemigrammus* aff. *vorderwinkleri*	piaba
Cypriniformes-Characo.	Characidae	*Hydrolycus scomberoides*	peixe-cachorro
Cypriniformes-Characo.	Characidae	*Hyphessobrycon* cf. *copelandi*	piaba
Cypriniformes-Characo.	Characidae	*Hyphessobrycon* gr. *bentosi*	piaba
Cypriniformes-Characo.	Characidae	*Hyphessobrycon heterorhabdus*	piaba
Cypriniformes-Characo.	Characidae	*Iguanodectes spilurus*	-
Cypriniformes-Characo.	Characidae	*Moenkhausia dichroura*	piaba
Cypriniformes-Characo.	Characidae	*Moenkhausia intermedia*	piaba
Cypriniformes-Characo.	Characidae	*Moenkhausia lepidura*	piaba
Cypriniformes-Characo.	Characidae	*Moenkhausia* gr. *lepidura* sp. 1	piaba
Cypriniformes-Characo.	Characidae	*Moenkhausia* gr. *lepidura* sp. 2	piaba
Cypriniformes-Characo.	Characidae	*Moenkhausia oligolepis*	piaba
Cypriniformes-Characo.	Characidae	*Phenacogaster* cf. *pectinatus*	-
Cypriniformes-Characo.	Characidae	*Prionobrama filigera*	-

GROUP	FAMILY	SPECIES NAME*	LOCAL NAMES
Cypriniformes-Characo.	Characidae	*Prionobrama* sp. 1	-
Cypriniformes-Characo.	Characidae	*Rhaphiodon vulpinus*	peixe-cachorro
Cypriniformes-Characo.	Characidae	*Roeboides myersi*	-
Cypriniformes-Characo.	Characidae	*Roeboides affinis*	-
Cypriniformes-Characo.	Characidae	*Saccoderma* sp. 1	piaba
Cypriniformes-Characo.	Characidae	*Stichonodon insignis*	piaba
Cypriniformes-Characo.	Characidae	*Tetragonopterus argenteus*	piaba
Cypriniformes-Characo.	Characidae	*Triportheus albus*	sardinha
Cypriniformes-Characo.	Characidae	*Triportheus angulatus*	sardinha-chata
Cypriniformes-Characo.	Characidae	*Triportheus elongatus*	sardinha-comprida
Gymnotiformes	Sternopygidae	*Sternopygus macrurus*	sarapó
Gymnotiformes	Sternopygidae	*Sternopygus* cf. *astrabes*	sarapó
Gymnotiformes	Gymnotidae	*Gymnotus anguillaris*	sarapó
Gymnotiformes	Gymnotidae	*Gymnotus* cf. *coatesi*	sarapó
Gymnotiformes	Gymnotidae	*Gymnotus* sp. nov. A	sarapó
Gymnotiformes	Gymnotidae	*Gymnotus* sp. nov. B	sarapó
Gymnotiformes	Gymnotidae	*Gymnotus* sp. nov. C	sarapó
Gymnotiformes	Gymnotidae	*Gymnotus* sp. nov. D	sarapó
Gymnotiformes	Gymnotidae	*Gymnotus* sp. nov. E	sarapó
Gymnotiformes	Gymnotidae	*Gymnotus* sp. 1	sarapó
Gymnotiformes	Electrophoridae	*Electrophorus electricus*	poraquê
Gymnotiformes	Rhamphichthyidae	*Rhamphichthys* sp. 1	sarapó
Gymnotiformes	Rhamphichthyidae	*Rhamphichthys* sp. 2	sarapó
Gymnotiformes	Rhamphichthyidae	*Gymnorhamphichthys rondoni*	sarapó
Gymnotiformes	Rhamphichthyidae	*Gymnorhamphichthys hypostomus*	sarapó
Gymnotiformes	Rhamphichthyidae	*Hypopygus lepturus*	sarapó
Gymnotiformes	Rhamphichthyidae	*Steatogenys elegans*	sarapó
Gymnotiformes	Rhamphichthyidae	*Steatogenys duidae*	sarapó
Gymnotiformes	Rhamphichthyidae	*Steatogenys* sp. nov. A	sarapó
Gymnotiformes	Hypopomidae	*Brachyhypopomus* sp. nov. A	sarapó
Gymnotiformes	Hypopomidae	*Brachyhypopomus beebei*	sarapó
Gymnotiformes	Hypopomidae	*Brachyhypopomus* sp. nov. B	sarapó
Gymnotiformes	Hypopomidae	*Brachyhypopomus* sp. nov. C	sarapó
Gymnotiformes	Hypopomidae	*Brachyhypopomus pinnicaudatus*	sarapó
Gymnotiformes	Hypopomidae	*Brachyhypopomus brevirostris*	sarapó
Gymnotiformes	Hypopomidae	*Brachyhypopomus* sp. nov. D	sarapó
Gymnotiformes	Hypopomidae	*Brachyhypopomus* sp. nov. E	sarapó
Gymnotiformes	Hypopomidae	*Brachyhypopomus* sp. nov. F	sarapó
Gymnotiformes	Hypopomidae	*Brachyhypopomus* sp. 1	sarapó
Gymnotiformes	Hypopomidae	*Microsternarchus bilineatus*	sarapó
Gymnotiformes	Eigenmanniidae	*Distocyclus conirostris*	sarapó
Gymnotiformes	Eigenmanniidae	*Eigenmannia limbata*	sarapó
Gymnotiformes	Eigenmanniidae	*Eigenmannia* cf. *virescens* (A)	sarapó
Gymnotiformes	Eigenmanniidae	*Eigenmannia* gr. *virescens* (B)	sarapó
Gymnotiformes	Apteronotidae	*Apteronotus hasemani*	sarapó
Gymnotiformes	Apteronotidae	*Apteronotus bonapartii*	sarapó
Gymnotiformes	Apteronotidae	*Apteronotus albifrons*	sarapó, ituí
Gymnotiformes	Apteronotidae	*Apteronotus anas*	sarapó
Gymnotiformes	Apteronotidae	*Porotergus gymnotus*	sarapó
Gymnotiformes	Apteronotidae	*Porotergus gimbeli*	sarapó
Gymnotiformes	Apteronotidae	*Porotergus compsus*	sarapó
Gymnotiformes	Apteronotidae	*Porotergus* sp. nov. A	sarapó
Gymnotiformes	Apteronotidae	*Platyurosternarchus macrostomus*	sarapó
Gymnotiformes	Apteronotidae	*Sternarchella schotti*	sarapó

GROUP	FAMILY	SPECIES NAME*	LOCAL NAMES
Gymnotiformes	Apteronotidae	*Sternarchella terminalis*	sarapó
Gymnotiformes	Apteronotidae	*Sternarchogiton porcinum*	sarapó
Gymnotiformes	Apteronotidae	*Sternarchogiton nattereri*	sarapó
Gymnotiformes	Apteronotidae	*Sternarchorhynchus oxyrhynchus*	sarapó
Gymnotiformes	Apteronotidae	*Sternarchorhynchus curvirostris*	sarapó
Gymnotiformes	Apteronotidae	*Sternarchorhynchus mormyrus*	sarapó
Gymnotiformes	Apteronotidae	*Sternarchorhamphus muelleri*	sarapó
Gymnotiformes	Apteronotidae	*Magosternarchus duccis*	sarapó
Gymnotiformes	Apteronotidae	*Orthosternarchus tamandua*	sarapó
Gymnotiformes	Apteronotidae	*Oedemognathus exodon*	sarapó
Siluriformes	Doradidae	*Acanthodoras cataphractus*	reque-reque
Siluriformes	Doradidae	*Acanthodoras spinosissimus*	reque-reque
Siluriformes	Doradidae	*Agamyxis pectinifrons*	reque-reque
Siluriformes	Doradidae	*Amblydoras hancocki*	reque-reque
Siluriformes	Doradidae	*Anadoras* cf. *regani*	reque-reque
Siluriformes	Doradidae	*Anduzedoras* sp. 1	reque-reque
Siluriformes	Doradidae	*Astrodoras* sp. 1	reque-reque
Siluriformes	Doradidae	*Centrodoras brachiatus*	reque-reque
Siluriformes	Doradidae	*Doras microstomas*	reque-reque
Siluriformes	Doradidae	*Doras fimbriatus*	reque-reque
Siluriformes	Doradidae	*Hassar* cf. *wilderi*	reque-reque
Siluriformes	Doradidae	*Hemidoras* sp. 1	reque-reque
Siluriformes	Doradidae	*Lithodoras dorsalis*	bacu-pedra
Siluriformes	Doradidae	*Megalodoras irwini*	rabeca, bacu-uruá
Siluriformes	Doradidae	*Opsodoras trimaculatus*	reque-reque
Siluriformes	Doradidae	*Opsodoras boulengeri*	reque-reque
Siluriformes	Doradidae	*Opsodoras humeralis*	reque-reque
Siluriformes	Doradidae	*Petalodoras* sp. 1	reque-reque
Siluriformes	Doradidae	*Petalodoras* sp. 2	reque-reque
Siluriformes	Doradidae	*Petalodoras* sp. 3	reque-reque
Siluriformes	Doradidae	*Platydoras costatus*	reque-reque
Siluriformes	Doradidae	*Pseudodoras niger*	cuiú-cuiú
Siluriformes	Doradidae	*Pterodoras granulosus*	bacuí
Siluriformes	Doradidae	*Rhyncodoras* cf. *xingui*	reque-reque
Siluriformes	Doradidae	*Scorpiodoras* cf. *heckelii*	reque-reque
Siluriformes	Doradidae	*Trachydoras atripes*	reque-reque
Siluriformes	Doradidae	*Trachydoras* cf. *paraguayensis*	reque-reque
Siluriformes	Doradidae	*Trachydoras* cf. *nattereri*	reque-reque
Siluriformes	Auchenipteridae	*Auchenipterichthys thoracatus*	cangati
Siluriformes	Auchenipteridae	*Auchenipterus nuchalis*	cangati
Siluriformes	Auchenipteridae	*Auchenipterus* sp. 1	cangati
Siluriformes	Auchenipteridae	*Centromochlus heckelii*	cangati
Siluriformes	Auchenipteridae	*Centromochlus* sp.	cangati
Siluriformes	Auchenipteridae	*Parauchenipterus galeatus*	cangati
Siluriformes	Auchenipteridae	*Pseudepapterus hasemani*	cangati
Siluriformes	Auchenipteridae	*Pseudauchenipterus* cf. *nodosus*	cangati
Siluriformes	Auchenipteridae	*Tatia* cf. *intermedia*	cangati
Siluriformes	Auchenipteridae	*Tatia* sp. 1	cangati
Siluriformes	Auchenipteridae	*Trachelyopterichthys taeniatus*	cangati
Siluriformes	Auchenipteridae	*Trachycorystes trachycorystes*	cangati
Siluriformes	Aspredinidae	*Agmus scabriceps*	rebeca banjo
Siluriformes	Aspredinidae	*Dysichthys* cf. *coracoideus*	rebeca banjo
Siluriformes	Aspredinidae	*Petacara dolichurus*	rebeca banjo
Siluriformes	Pimelodidae	*Bathypotamichthys* sp.	-

GROUP	FAMILY	SPECIES NAME*	LOCAL NAMES
Siluriformes	Pimelodidae	*Brachyglanis* sp. 1	-
Siluriformes	Pimelodidae	*Brachyplatystoma filamentosum*	filhote, piraíba
Siluriformes	Pimelodidae	*Brachyplatystoma flavicans*	dourada
Siluriformes	Pimelodidae	*Brachyplatystoma vaillantii*	piramutaba
Siluriformes	Pimelodidae	*Brachyplatystoma juruense*	zebra
Siluriformes	Pimelodidae	*Calophysus macropterus*	piracatinga
Siluriformes	Pimelodidae	*Exallodontus aguanai*	-
Siluriformes	Pimelodidae	*Goeldiella eques*	mandi
Siluriformes	Pimelodidae	*Goslinia platynema*	babão
Siluriformes	Pimelodidae	*Hemisorubim platyrhynchos*	braço-de-moça
Siluriformes	Pimelodidae	*Leiarius marmoratus*	jandiá
Siluriformes	Pimelodidae	*Leiarius pictus*	-
Siluriformes	Pimelodidae	*Megalonema* sp.	-
Siluriformes	Pimelodidae	*Microglanis* cf. *iheringi*	-
Siluriformes	Pimelodidae	*Paulicea luetkeni*	jaú, pacamum
Siluriformes	Pimelodidae	*Phractocephalus hemioliopterus*	pirarara
Siluriformes	Pimelodidae	*Pimelodella* cf. *cristata*	mandi
Siluriformes	Pimelodidae	*Pimelodina* cf. *flavipinnis*	mandi
Siluriformes	Pimelodidae	*Pimelodus altipinnis*	mandi
Siluriformes	Pimelodidae	*Pimelodus blochii*	mandi
Siluriformes	Pimelodidae	*Pimelodus* sp. 1	mandi
Siluriformes	Pimelodidae	*Pinirampus pirinampu*	barba-chata, piranambu
Siluriformes	Pimelodidae	*Platynematichthys notatus*	-
Siluriformes	Pimelodidae	*Platystomatichthys sturio*	mandi
Siluriformes	Pimelodidae	*Pseudopimelodus raninus*	mandi
Siluriformes	Pimelodidae	*Pseudoplatystoma fasciatum*	surubim
Siluriformes	Pimelodidae	*Pseudoplatystoma tigrinum*	caparari
Siluriformes	Pimelodidae	*Sorubim lima*	bico-de-pato
Siluriformes	Pimelodidae	*Sorubimichthys planiceps*	peixe-lenha
Siluriformes	Pimelodidae	*Rhamdia* cf. *quelen*	mandi
Siluriformes	Ageneiosidae	*Ageneiosus vittatus*	mandubé
Siluriformes	Ageneiosidae	*Ageneiosus brevifilis*	mandubé, bocudo
Siluriformes	Ageneiosidae	*Ageneiosus* sp.	mandubé
Siluriformes	Ageneiosidae	*Tympanopleura* cf. *alta*	mandubé
Siluriformes	Helogeneidae	*Helogenes* cf. *marmoratus*	-
Siluriformes	Cetopsidae	*Cetopsis coecutiens*	candiru-açu
Siluriformes	Hypophthalmidae	*Hypophthalmus edentatus*	mapará
Siluriformes	Hypophthalmidae	*Hypophthalmus fimbriatus*	mapará
Siluriformes	Hypophthalmidae	*Hypophthalmus marginatus*	mapará
Siluriformes	Trichomycteridae	*Eremophilus candidus*	candiru
Siluriformes	Trichomycteridae	*Pareiodon microps*	candiru
Siluriformes	Trichomycteridae	*Pseudostegophilus nemurus*	candiru
Siluriformes	Trichomycteridae	*Pseudostegophilus* sp. 1	candiru
Siluriformes	Trichomycteridae	*Vandellia* sp. 1	candiru
Siluriformes	Trichomycteridae	Trichomycteridae sp. indet. 1	candiru
Siluriformes	Callichthyidae	*Corydoras* sp. 1	tamoatá
Siluriformes	Callichthyidae	*Dianemis longibarbus*	tamoatá
Siluriformes	Callichthyidae	*Hoplosternum thoracatum*	tamoatá
Siluriformes	Callichthyidae	*Hoplosternum littorale*	tamoatá
Siluriformes	Callichthyidae	*Hoplosternum* sp. 1	tamoatá
Siluriformes	Callichthyidae	*Callichthys callichthys*	tamoatá
Siluriformes	Loricariidae	*Ancistrus* cf. *hoplogenys*	acari
Siluriformes	Loricariidae	*Ancistrus* sp.	acari
Siluriformes	Loricariidae	*Dekeyseria scaphirhyncha*	acari

GROUP	FAMILY	SPECIES NAME*	LOCAL NAMES
Siluriformes	Loricariidae	*Farlowella amazona*	acari-chato
Siluriformes	Loricariidae	*Farlowella henrique*	acari-chato
Siluriformes	Loricariidae	*Farlowella nattereri*	acari-chato
Siluriformes	Loricariidae	*Hemiodontichthys acipenserinus*	acari
Siluriformes	Loricariidae	*Hypoptopoma* cf. *gulare*	acari
Siluriformes	Loricariidae	*Hypoptopoma* sp.	acari
Siluriformes	Loricariidae	*Hypostomus carinatus*	bodó
Siluriformes	Loricariidae	*Hypostomus* cf. *emarginatus*	bodó
Siluriformes	Loricariidae	*Liposarcus multiradiatus*	bodó
Siluriformes	Loricariidae	*Loricarichthys acutus*	acari
Siluriformes	Loricariidae	*Loricarichthys maculatus*	acari-bodó
Siluriformes	Loricariidae	*Loricarichthys nudirostris*	acari
Siluriformes	Loricariidae	*Oxyropsis* cf. *acutirostris*	acari
Siluriformes	Loricariidae	*Peckoltia* cf. *brevis*	bodó
Siluriformes	Loricariidae	*Pseudorinelepis* cf. *pellegrini*	bodó
Siluriformes	Loricariidae	*Pterygoplichthys gibbiceps*	acari-pedra
Siluriformes	Loricariidae	*Rineloricaria lanceolata*	acari
Siluriformes	Loricariidae	*Rineloricaria* sp.	acari
Atheriniformes	Belonidae	*Potamorrhaphis guianensis*	peixe-agulha
Atheriniformes	Belonidae	*Pseudotylosurus microps*	peixe-agulha
Atheriniformes	Cyprinodontidae	*Fluviphylax* cf. *pygmaeus*	-
Atheriniformes	Cyprinodontidae	*Rivulus* sp. 1	-
Atheriniformes	Cyprinodontidae	*Rivulus* sp. 2	-
Synbranchiformes	Synbranchidae	*Synbranchus marmoratus*	muçum-pintado
Synbranchiformes	Synbranchidae	*Synbranchus* sp. 1	muçum-cinzo
Perciformes	Sciaenidae	*Pachypops furcraeus*	pescada
Perciformes	Sciaenidae	*Plagioscon squamosissimus*	pescada
Perciformes	Sciaenidae	*Plagioscon* sp.	pescada
Perciformes	Cichlidae	*Acarichthys heckelii*	acará
Perciformes	Cichlidae	*Acaronia nassa*	acará-lanterna
Perciformes	Cichlidae	*Aeguidens diadema*	acará
Perciformes	Cichlidae	*Aequidens tetramerus*	acará-bocudo
Perciformes	Cichlidae	*Apistogrammoides pucallpaensis*	acará
Perciformes	Cichlidae	*Apistogramma* cf. *agassizii*	acará
Perciformes	Cichlidae	*Apistogramma* sp. 1	acará
Perciformes	Cichlidae	*Astronotus ocellatus*	acará-açu
Perciformes	Cichlidae	*Biotodoma cupido*	acará
Perciformes	Cichlidae	*Chaetobranchus semifasicatus*	acará-tucunaré
Perciformes	Cichlidae	*Chaetobranchus flavescens*	acará-branca
Perciformes	Cichlidae	*Cichla monoculus*	tucunaré
Perciformes	Cichlidae	*Crenicichla reticulata*	jacundá
Perciformes	Cichlidae	*Crenicichla johanna*	jacundá
Perciformes	Cichlidae	*Crenicichla cincta*	jacundá
Perciformes	Cichlidae	*Crenicichla* gr. *lugubris*	jacundá-vermelha
Perciformes	Cichlidae	*Crenicichla* cf. *labrina*	jacundá
Perciformes	Cichlidae	*Cichlasoma amazonarum*	acará
Perciformes	Cichlidae	*Geophagus proximus*	acará roe-roe
Perciformes	Cichlidae	*Heros appendiculatus*	acará-roxo
Perciformes	Cichlidae	*Hypselecara temporalis*	acará
Perciformes	Cichlidae	*Mesonauta insignis*	acará-boari
Perciformes	Cichlidae	*Pterophyllum scalare*	acará-bandeira
Perciformes	Cichlidae	*Satanoperca jurupari*	acará-garrafa
Perciformes	Cichlidae	*Symphysodon aequifasciatus*	acará-disco
Perciformes	Cichlidae	*Uaru amphiacanthoides*	acará-bararuá

GROUP	FAMILY	SPECIES NAME*	LOCAL NAMES
Perciformes	Gobiidae	*Mycrophylipus* sp.	-
Perciformes	Nandidae	*Monocirrhus polyacanthus*	peixe-folha
Pleuronectiformes	Soleidae	*Achirus* sp.	soia, solha
Tetraodontiformes	Tetraodontidae	*Colomesus asellus*	baiacu
ARTROPODA			
CRUSTACEA			
Malacostraca			
Decapoda		*Macrobrachium amazonicum*	camarão
Decapoda		*Palaemonetes ivinicus*	camarão
Decapoda		*Euryrhinchus amazoniensis*	camarão
Decapoda		*Sylviocarcinus pictus*	caranguejo
Decapoda		*Dilocarcinus pagei*	caranguejo
Decapoda		*Trichodactylus faxoni*	camarão
Decapoda		*Fredilocarcinus* sp. nov.	caranguejo
Mysidacea		*Parvimysis pisciscebus*	-
INSECTA			
Lepdoptera			
Rhopalocera	Nymphalidae	*Morpho achilles*	-
Rhopalocera	Nymphalidae	*Morpho menelaus*	-
Rhopalocera	Nymphalidae	*Caligo teucer*	-
Rhopalocera	Nymphalidae	*Caligo illioneus*	-
Rhopalocera	Nymphalidae	*Philaethria dido*	-
Rhopalocera	Nymphalidae	*Heliconius pardalinus*	-
Rhopalocera	Nymphalidae	*Heliconius melpomene aglaope*	-
Rhopalocera	Nymphalidae	*Laparus doris*	-
Rhopalocera	Nymphalidae	*Heliconius sara thamar*	-
Rhopalocera	Nymphalidae	*Heliconius antiochus*	-
Rhopalocera	Nymphalidae	*Dryadula phaetusa*	-
Rhopalocera	Nymphalidae	*Anartia amathea*	-
Rhopalocera	Nymphalidae	*Anartia jatrophae*	-
Rhopalocera	Nymphalidae	*Opsiphanes invirae*	-
Rhopalocera	Nymphalidae	*Opsiphanes berecynthia*	-
Rhopalocera	Nymphalidae	*Biblis hyperia*	-
Rhopalocera	Nymphalidae	*Historis odius*	-
Rhopalocera	Nymphalidae	*Historis acheronta*	-
Rhopalocera	Nymphalidae	*Agrias amydon*	-
Rhopalocera	Nymphalidae	*Prepona demophon*	-
Rhopalocera	Nymphalidae	*Prepona demophoon*	-
Rhopalocera	Nymphalidae	*Prepona laertes*	-
Rhopalocera	Nymphalidae	*Colobura dirce*	-
Rhopalocera	Nymphalidae	*Hamadryas feronia*	-
Rhopalocera	Nymphalidae	*Hamadryas laodamia*	-
Rhopalocera	Nymphalidae	*Paulograma peristera*	-
Rhopalocera	Nymphalidae	*Tigridia acesta*	-
Rhopalocera	Nymphalidae	*Pyrrhogyra crameri*	-
Rhopalocera	Nymphalidae	*Lycorea pasinuntia*	-
Rhopalocera	Nymphalidae	*Mechanitis polymnia*	-
Rhopalocera	Nymphalidae	*Mechanitis mazeus*	-

GROUP	FAMILY	SPECIES NAME*	LOCAL NAMES
Rhopalocera	Nymphalidae	*Melinaea maelus*	-
Rhopalocera	Nymphalidae	*Melinaea maenius*	-
Rhopalocera	Nymphalidae	*Melinaea ludovica*	-
Rhopalocera	Nymphalidae	*Hypothyris fluonia*	-
Rhopalocera	Nymphalidae	*Tithorea harmonia egaensis*	-
Rhopalocera	Nymphalidae	*Pierella lamia chalybaea*	-
Rhopalocera	Nymphalidae	*Pteronymia vestilla*	-
Rhopalocera	Nymphalidae	*Danaus eresimus*	-
Rhopalocera	Nymphalidae	*Catonephele antinoe*	-
Rhopalocera	Nymphalidae	*Eunica amelia*	-
Rhopalocera	Nymphalidae	*Hypna clytemnestra*	-
Rhopalocera	Nymphalidae	*Zaretis itys*	-
Rhopalocera	Nymphalidae	*Doxocopa agathina*	-
Rhopalocera	Nymphalidae	*Adelpha thoasa*	-
Rhopalocera	Nymphalidae	*Posttaygetis penelea*	-
Rhopalocera	Nymphalidae	*Cissia herseis*	-
Rhopalocera	Nymphalidae	*Caeruleuptychia* sp.	-
Rhopalocera	Nymphalidae	*Hermeuptychia hermes*	-
Rhopalocera	Nymphalidae	*Splendeuptychia quadrina*	-
Rhopalocera	Nymphalidae	*Harjesia blanda*	-
Rhopalocera	Nymphalidae	*Taygetis erubescens*	-
Rhopalocera	Nymphalidae	*Pseudodebis valentina*	-
Rhopalocera	Nymphalidae	*Pareuptychia summandosa*	-
Rhopalocera	Nymphalidae	*Chloreuptychia herseis*	-
Rhopalocera	Nymphalidae	*Mazia amazonica*	-
Rhopalocera	Papilionidae	*Parides neophilus olivencius*	-
Rhopalocera	Papilionidae	*Heraclides chiansiades*	-
Rhopalocera	Pieridae	*Phoebis sennae*	-
Rhopalocera	Pieridae	*Phoebis philea*	-
Rhopalocera	Pieridae	*Phoebis argante*	-
Rhopalocera	Pieridae	*Phoebis trite*	-
Rhopalocera	Pieridae	*Ascia monuste*	-
Rhopalocera	Pieridae	*Ascia buniae*	-
Rhopalocera	Pieridae	*Apias drusilla*	-
Rhopalocera	Pieridae	*Eurema leuce*	-
Rhopalocera	Pieridae	*Eurema albula*	-
Rhopalocera	Lycaenidae	*Helicopis cupido*	-
Rhopalocera	Lycaenidae	*Helicopis gnidus*	-
Rhopalocera	Lycaenidae	*Riodina lysippus*	-
Rhopalocera	Lycaenidae	*Panara phereclus*	-
Rhopalocera	Hesperiidae	*Bangalotis astylos*	-
Rhopalocera	Hesperiidae	*Augiades crinisus*	-
Rhopalocera	Hesperiidae	*Zenis jebus*	-
Rhopalocera	Hesperiidae	*Urbanus simplicius*	-
Heterocera	Saturniidae	*Rothschildia erycina*	-
Heterocera	Saturniidae	*Arsenura ciocolatina*	-
Heterocera	Sphingidae	*Perigonia* sp.	-
Heterocera	Sphingidae	*Pseudosphinx tetrio*	-
Heterocera	Uraniidae	*Urania leilus*	-

GROUP	FAMILY	SPECIES NAME*	LOCAL NAMES
ZOOPLANKTON			
ROTIFERA			
Monogonta		*Beauchampia crucigera*	-
Monogonta		*Beauchampeilla eudactylota*	-
Monogonta/Ploina	Brachionidae	*Brachionus falcatus*	-
Monogonta/Ploina	Brachionidae	*Brachionus gessner*	-
Monogonta/Ploina	Brachionidae	*Brachionus mirabilis*	-
Monogonta/Ploina	Brachionidae	*Brachionus patulus*	-
Monogonta/Ploina	Brachionidae	*Brachionus zahniseri*	-
Monogonta/Ploina	Brachionidae	*Brachionus mirus* var. *voigti*	-
Monogonta/Ploina	Brachionidae	*Brachionus caudatus*	-
Monogonta/Ploina	Brachionidae	*Dipleuchlanis propatula*	-
Monogonta/Ploina	Brachionidae	*Euchlanis incisa*	-
Monogonta/Ploina	Brachionidae	*Euchlanis dilatata liucksiana*	-
Monogonta/Ploina	Brachionidae	*Euchlanis meneta*	-
Monogonta/Ploina	Brachionidae	*Euchlanis deflexa*	-
Monogonta/Ploina	Brachionidae	*Keratella americana*	-
Monogonta/Ploina	Brachionidae	*Keratella coclearis*	-
Monogonta/Ploina	Brachionidae	*Keratella lenzi*	-
Monogonta/Ploina	Brachionidae	*Macrochaetus multispinosa*	-
Monogonta/Ploina	Brachionidae	*Macrochaetus linsi*	-
Monogonta/Ploina	Brachionidae	*Macrochaetus acantophora*	-
Monogonta/Ploina	Brachionidae	*Mytilina sinatherina socialis*	-
Monogonta/Ploina	Brachionidae	*Platyias leloupi*	-
Monogonta/Ploina	Brachionidae	*Platyias quadricornis*	-
Monogonta/Ploina	Trichocercidae	*Trichocerca collaris*	-
Monogonta/Ploina	Trichocercidae	*Trichocerca collaris*	-
Monogonta/Ploina	Trichocercidae	*Trichocerca similis*	-
Monogonta/Ploina	Trichocercidae	*Trichocerca tenuior*	-
Monogonta/Ploina	Trichocercidae	*Trichocerca weberi*	-
Monogonta/Ploina	Lecaninae	*Lecane bulla*	-
Monogonta/Ploina	Lecaninae	*Lecane cornuta*	-
Monogonta/Ploina	Lecaninae	*Lecane curvicornis*	-
Monogonta/Ploina	Lecaninae	*Lecane leontina*	-
Monogonta/Ploina	Lecaninae	*Lecane ludwigi*	-
Monogonta/Ploina	Lecaninae	*Lecane luna*	-
Monogonta/Ploina	Lecaninae	*Lecane papuana*	-
Monogonta/Ploina	Lecaninae	*Lecane ohioensis*	-
Monogonta/Ploina	Lecaninae	*Lecane quadricornis*	-
Monogonta/Ploina	Flosculariidae	*Beauchapia crucigera*	-
Monogonta/Ploina	Flosculariidae	*Beauchampeilla eudactylota*	-
Monogonta/Ploina	Flosculariidae	*Floscularia ringens*	-
Monogonta/Ploina	Flosculariidae	*Limnias ceratophylii*	-
Monogonta/Ploina	Flosculariidae	*Limnias melicerta*	-
Monogonta/Ploina	Hexarthridae	*Hehaarthra brasiliensis*	-
Monogonta/Ploina	Testudinellidae	*Testudinella patina*	-
Monogonta/Ploina	Testudinellidae	*Testudinella hauriensis*	-
Monogonta/Ploina	Testudinellidae	*Filinia saltator*	-
Monogonta/Ploina	Testudinellidae	*Filinia* sp.	-
Monogonta/Ploina	Notommatidae	*Cephalodella* sp.	-
Monogonta/Ploina	Notommatidae	*Eosphora anthadis*	-
Monogonta/Ploina	Notommatidae	*Proales* sp.	-

GROUP	FAMILY	SPECIES NAME*	LOCAL NAMES
Monogonta/Ploina	Notommatidae	*Lindia truncata*	-
Monogonta/Ploina	Notommatidae	*Dicranophorus caudatus*	-
Monogonta/Ploina	Notommatidae	*Collotheca ornata*	-
Monogonta/Ploina	Notommatidae	*Scaridium longicauda*	-
Digononta		*Bdelloidea* sp.	-
Digononta		*Dissotrocha aculeata*	-
Digononta		*Dissotrocha macrostyla*	-
Digononta		*Dissotrocha schlienzi*	-
Digononta		*Rotatoria rotaria*	-
Digononta		*Rotatoria neptunia*	-
Digononta		*Asplanchna* sp.	-
Digononta		*Trochosphaera* sp.	-
Digononta/Anopoda	Daphnidae	*Ceriodaphnia* cf. *cornuta*	-
Digononta/Anopoda	Daphnidae	*Ceriodaphnia coregoni rigaudi*	-
Digononta/Anopoda	Daphnidae	*Ceriodapnhia reticulata*	-
Digononta/Anopoda	Moinidae	*Moinodaphnia macleayi*	-
Digononta/Anopoda	Moinidae	*Moina reticulata*	-
Digononta/Anopoda	Moinidae	*Moina minuta*	-
Digononta/Anopoda	Bosminidae	*Bosmina* sp.	-
Digononta/Anopoda	Bosminidae	*Bosminopsis macaguensis*	-
Digononta/Anopoda	Bosminidae	*Bosminopsis deitersi*	-
Digononta/Anopoda	Ilyocryptidae	*Ilyocryptus spinifer*	-
Digononta/Anopoda	Macrothricidae	*Grimaldina brazzai*	-
Digononta/Anopoda	Macrothricidae	*Macrothr* sp.	-
Digononta/Ctenopoda	Sididae	*Diaphanosoma polyspina*	-
Digononta/Ctenopoda	Sididae	*Sarsilatona serricauda*	-
Digononta/Ctenopoda	Sididae	*Diaphanosoma* sp.	-
Digononta/Copepoda			
Calanoida	Diaptomidae	*"Diaptomus" ohlei* (?)	-
Calanoida	Diaptomidae	*Dactylodiaptomus pearsie*	-
Calanoida	Diaptomidae	*Dactylodiaptomus coronatus*	-
Calanoida	Diaptomidae	*Notodiaptomus amazonicus*	-
Calanoida	Diaptomidae	*Notodiaptomus coniferoides*	-
Calanoida	Diaptomidae	*Notodiaptomus kieferi*	-
Calanoida	Diaptomidae	*Rhacodiaptomus besti*	-
Cyclopoida		*Mesocyclops braziliensis*	-
Cyclopoida		*Mesocyclops longisetus*	-
Cyclopoida		*Macrocyclops albinus*	-
Cyclopoida		*Macrocyclops cebaceus*	-
Cyclopoida		*Macrocyclops finitunus*	-
Cyclopoida		*Thermocyclops tenuis*	-

* Some of the species listed here are under taxonomic dispute, and can not be allocated in one particular higher group or even family, or the higher *taxon* is unknown by the specialist.

4- SUGGESTED FURTHER READINGS

AYRES, José Márcio. *As matas de várzea do Mamirauá*. Brasília, DF: Sociedade Civil Mamirauá, CNPq/PTU. Série Estudos do Mamirauá, v. 1, 124 p., 1995.

GOULDING, Michael. *Amazon*: the flooded forest. London: BBC Books. 208 p., 1989.

LIMA, Deborah M. A implantação de uma unidade de conservação em área de várzea: a experiência de Mamirauá. *In*: *A Amazônia e a crise da modernização*. D' INCAO, M. Angela & SILVEIRA, I. Maciel da (Org.). Belém: MPEG, 1994.

PADOCH, Christine, AYRES, José Márcio, PINEDO-VASQUEZ, Miguel & HENDERSON, Andrew (Ed.). *Várzea*: diversity, development, and conservation of Amazonia's whitewater floodplains. New York: New York Botanical Garden Press. 407 p., 1999.

QUEIROZ, Helder L. & CRAMPTON, William G. R. (Ed.). *Estratégias para manejo de recursos pesqueiros em Mamirauá*. Brasília, DF: Sociedade Civil Mamirauá, MCT-CNPq. Série Estudos do Mamirauá, v. 5, 198 p., 1999.

SOCIEDADE Civil Mamirauá. *Mamirauá Management Plan*. Brasília, DF. 96 p., 1996.

Obs.: many other Mamirauá Publications books are found at http://www.pop-tefe.rnp.br

Printed in Brazil

Color separations:
Ponto & Cor
Rio de Janeiro

Printing:
Gráfica Assaré
Rio de Janeiro

IDSM

Av. Brasil, 197 - Bairro Juruá
Caixa Postal 38 - CEP 69470-000
Tefé - AM - Brazil
Phone: (92) 343-4672 / 343-2736
Fax: (92) 343-2736